MIKE LEIGH

Dramatist and director in theatre, film and television, Mike Leigh was born in 1943 in Salford, Lancashire. He trained at the Royal Academy of Dramatic Art, at Camberwell and Central Art Schools, and at the London Film School. He went on to gain wide acting, directing and designing skills at various theatres, including a season with the Royal Shakespeare Company.

His first original play, *The Box Play*, evolved under his direction at the Midlands Arts Centre in Birmingham in 1965, and he has continued to use this method of creating a script for theatre or film from extensive extemporised rehearsals.

Subsequent stage plays include *Bleak Moments* at the Open Space Theatre, London, *Wholesome Glory* (Royal Court, 1973), *Babies Grow Old* (RSC, 1974) and four first seen at Hampstead Theatre: *Abigail's Party* (1977), *Ecstasy* (1979), *Goose Pimples* (1981) and *Smelling a Rat* (1988). More recently *Greek Tragedy* (1990) and *It's a Great Big Shame!* (1993) were seen in London at the Theatre Royal, Stratford East.

After developing *Bleak Moments* as a film in 1971, Leigh's work for television and film includes *Hard Labour* (1972), *Nuts in May* (1975), *The Kiss of Death* (1976), *Abigail's Party* (1977) *Who's Who* (1978), *Grown-Ups* 1980), *Home Sweet Home* (1982), *Meantime* (1983), *Four Days in July* (1985), *The Short and Curlies* (1987), *High Hopes* (1988), *Life is Sweet* (1990), *Naked* (1993: Best Direction Award, Cannes Film Festival) and *Secrets and Lies* (1996: Palme d'Or, Cannes). For radio, his work includes *Too Much of a Good Thing* (1992).

A Selection of Other Titles in This Series

Simon Block
NOT A GAME FOR BOYS

Howard Brenton
BERLIN BERTIE
H.I.D. (HESS IS DEAD)

Howard Brenton/Tariq Ali
IRANIAN NIGHTS
MOSCOW GOLD

Jez Butterworth
MOJO

Caryl Churchill
CHURCHILL: SHORTS
CLOUD NINE
ICECREAM
LIGHT SHINING IN
    BUCKINGHAMSHIRE
MAD FOREST
THE SKRIKER
TRAPS

Jean Cocteau
LES PARENTS TERRIBLES

Ariel Dorfman
DEATH AND THE
    MAIDEN
READER

David Edgar
PENTECOST
THE SHAPE OF THE
    TABLE

Kevin Elyot
MY NIGHT WITH REG

Peter Flannery
SINGER

Pam Gems
DEBORAH'S DAUGHTER
STANLEY

Stephen Jeffreys
THE CLINK
A GOING CONCERN
THE LIBERTINE

Larry Kramer
THE DESTINY OF ME
THE NORMAL HEART

Tony Kushner
ANGELS IN AMERICA
    PARTS ONE AND TWO
SLAvS!

Mike Leigh
ECSTASY

Doug Lucie
GRACE

Clare McIntyre
MY HEARTS A SUITCASE
    & LOW LEVEL PANIC
THE THICKNESS OF
    SKIN

Conor McPherson
THIS LIME TREE BOWER

Ludmila Petrushevskaya
CINZANO

Billy Roche
THE CAVALCADERS
THE WEXFORD
    TRILOGY

Diane Samuels
KINDERTRANSPORT

Seneca (trans. Churchill)
THYESTES

Claire Tomalin
THE WINTER WIFE

Mike Leigh

SMELLING A RAT

NICK HERN BOOKS
London

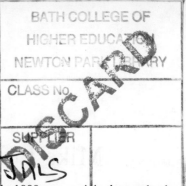

A Nick Hern Book

Smelling a Rat first published in 1989 as an original paperback
by Nick Hern Books. This edition first published in 1996 by
Nick Hern Books, 14 Larden Road, London W3 7ST

Front cover illustration of Mike Leigh by Antony Sher,
'Another Session' crayons, 1980. Reproduced with permission

Typeset by Book Ens, Saffron Walden, Essex
Printed by Athenaeum Press Ltd, Gateshead, Tyne and Wear

ISBN 1 85459 316 1

A CIP catalogue record for this book is available from
the British Library

Characters

REX
VIC
CHARMAINE
ROCK
MELANIE-JANE

The action takes place in Rex's bedroom on the day after Boxing Day.

ACT ONE   Late at night

ACT TWO   A few moments later

Time – the present

Smelling A Rat was first performed at the Hampstead Theatre, London on 6 December 1988 with the following cast:

REX	Eric Allan
VIC	Timothy Spall
CHARMAINE	Brid Brennan
ROCK	Greg Cruttwell
MELANIE-JANE	Saskia Reeves

Directed by Mike Leigh
Designed by Eve Stewart
Lighting by Kevin Sleep
Sound by John Leonard

ACT ONE

REX and Mrs Weasel's bedroom in their flat, which is on the fourth floor of an expensive penthouse-style modern block.

Built-in wardrobes, into which are recessed a king-size bed and a dressing-table. Pink, gold, silk and bows abound everywhere, but the dressing-table is cluttered and untidy.

On the bed, a carefully-arranged group of at least a dozen assorted soft 'cuddly' toys, including a Kermit the Frog, a Roland Rat, and several rodents, including a large mouse.

Door to main living area beyond, in which are visible a shelf-unit containing various ornaments and other artefacts, including a Spanish bull and some sporting trophies; also visible, part of the stereo system and some tapes and records. The rest of the flat unseen.

Above a bedside-table, a small fire-extinguisher is attached to the alcove; on this bedside-table a large torch, a telephone, a digital alarm-clock. On the other side, a radio/cassette-player, a 'Teasmade', some pill bottles.

Television set and two Spanish dolls on a chest of drawers; a blanket chest; an exercise-bike; an electric golf-putting practiser, with several of its balls lying around it on the floor; a sheepskin rug.

An adjacent en suite bathroom with sliding, frosted-glass door, and carpeted wall-to-wall, as is the whole room.

Before Lights Up, i.e. for the Pre-Set, the room is empty, and the door is closed. Darkness, broken only by the suggestion of moonlight through a Venetian blind.

Lights Up. Bright, theatrical music, evoking French farce.

The door opens immediately. REX *puts on the light and enters, briskly, with a duty-free carrier-bag and an airline shoulder-bag; he puts these on the bed. He picks up the torch, turns it on, and quickly inspects the floor of each wardrobe (for mouse-droppings), closing the door after each inspection. He turns off the torch, replaces it, and takes off his raincoat, which he hangs in the wardrobe situated between the door and the bed, closing the wardrobe door. He is wearing loud golfing-clothes, including a cap, which he keeps on throughout the play.*

His luggage can be seen through the doorway; this consists of a suitcase and a bag of golf-clubs; he now brings the latter into the room, checks it over, and places it carefully and lovingly in the same wardrobe.

He gets the suitcase, puts it on the blanket-chest, opens it, and takes out a silk dressing-gown and a toilet-bag; he goes to the bathroom, opens the door, puts on the light, goes in, deposits the gown and the bag, turns out the light, comes out, and closes the door.

Then he efficiently unpacks his shirts, underwear, pyjamas, woollens, handkerchiefs etc. into the chest of drawers, systematically filling one drawer at a time, one after the other. Then he places the suitcase in an overhead cupboard.

By now, the comic music should have finished.

He takes from the airline bag a hip-flask, which he puts on the bed. He puts the airline bag in the wardrobe, and takes the duty-free bag out of the room. He puts out the light in the other room. He comes back into the bedroom and puts on the bedside wall-light. He turns off the main light. He sits on the bed. He takes a swig from the hip-flask, heaves an end-of-hard-day sigh, and puts the flask on the bedside-table.

He picks up a soft toy, looks at it aggressively, and throws it on the floor in the centre of the room. He repeats this with the whole lot, giving some more attention than others, and some none at all, until the bed is clear, and the floor is strewn with cuddly bodies.

He has finished up in a kneeling position on the bed, in order to reach the furthest toys. He stops dead. Muffled talking is heard, off. He springs to the door stealthily, opens it ajar, and listens for a moment. Voices. Somebody turns on the light in the room beyond. He closes the door, and turns off the wall-light.

Pause. Then he gets into the golf-clubs wardrobe, and closes the door. He gets out, takes an airgun out of the bedside drawer, and gets back into the wardrobe, closing the door again.

Only now do we start to register clearly what we can hear, but for practical purposes here is everything that goes on offstage, starting as REX *is disposing of the last of the toys.*

CHARMAINE (*off*). I'll just wait 'ere, Vic.

VIC (*off*). Nah – come on . . .

CHARMAINE (*off*). No!

VIC (*off*). Come on!

Pause.

CHARMAINE (*off*). Is there a switch?

VIC (*off*). Can't see nothing.

CHARMAINE (*off*). There must be one.

VIC (*off*). Oh, 'ere it is – got it! (*Switches light on.*) That's it – bit of light on the subject. Shut the door, then!

CHARMAINE (*off*). You shut it.

VIC (*off*). Arr, there's nothing to worry about!

CHARMAINE (*off*). You 'ave to be careful.

VIC (*off*). There's another switch 'ere. (*Switches another light on.*) Cor', look a' this . . .

CHARMAINE (*off*). I'll just wait 'ere, Vic.

VIC (*off*). Nah, come on.

CHARMAINE (*off*). No.

By this time, REX *is in the wardrobe with the gun.*

VIC (*off*). It's alright for some, init? Money goes to money!

CHARMAINE (*off*). What's it like?

VIC (*off*). Bleedin' 'uge.

CHARMAINE (*off*). Oh! Init lovely?!

VIC (*off*). Well, it don't look like nothing's out of order.

CHARMAINE (*off*). It looks like 'Dynasty'!

VIC (*off*). Inasmuch as these windows ain't been tampered with.

CHARMAINE (*off*). The kitchen's small, in compromise to the lounge.

VIC (*off*). There's another room 'ere. (*He opens the bedroom door, and shines the torch at the exercise-bike*). Oh, look, Charmaine: Weasel's got a gym in 'is flat, the old fart!

CHARMAINE (*entering, she is eating something*). Don't shout, Vic.

VIC. Inasmuch as 'e's got to keep fit for 'is golfin' and sportin' activities.

CHARMAINE. I thought something was wrong.

VIC *shines the torch on the bed.*

VIC. 'E's got a bed in 'ere, an' all.

CHARMAINE. It's 'is bedroom.

VIC. Oh yeah, course it is. (*He shines the torch on the toys.*) What's all that gubbins all over the floor?

CHARMAINE. It's toys, init? 'As 'e got kids?

VIC. Yeah, 'e's got a son.

CHARMAINE. Oh, yeah.

VIC. 'Ang on, 'e's grown up.

CHARMAINE. Well 'e must 'ave grandchildren.

VIC. I don't think 'is boy's old enough to 'ave nippers. (*Pause.*) What're you eatin'?

CHARMAINE. Nothing!

VIC (*shining torch at her*). Yes, you are!

CHARMAINE. 'T's only a bit o' cookin' chocolate.

VIC. What, you nicked it?

CHARMAINE. Well, they'll never know.

VIC. It's all over your face.

CHARMAINE. Is it?!

VIC. Yeah. – No it ain't!

They both laugh, as they will many times throughout the play.
CHARMAINE*'s laugh is a crescendo of a giggle, good-humoured and generous, and not the least bit silly.* VIC*'s laugh might be said to resemble a bark* ('da!'), *but again it has a warmth. It isn't wicked or malevolent.*

CHARMAINE. Turn the light on, Vic – where's the switch?

VIC. There it is.

CHARMAINE. Oh, yeah.

VIC *turns on the light.*

CHARMAINE *gasps.*

VIC. Cor! Plush. (*Pause.*) Well, it don't look like it's been done over.

CHARMAINE. No.

VIC. Inasmuch the blagger nowadays, 'e ain't content with 'alf-inching yer personals, 'e's got to slice up yer furniture with a Stanley knife, and smear shit all over yer walls.

They both laugh.

CHARMAINE. There's Roland Rat!

VIC (*uninterested*). Yeah.

CHARMAINE. They're all the same, in't they, Vic?

VIC. They are.

CHARMAINE. Fancy going away and leaving your place like this.

VIC. 'E probably left in a 'urry.

CHARMAINE. When's 'e coming back?

VIC. End o' the week, I think.

CHARMAINE. Got a lot of wardrobes.

VIC. Yeah. Oh look, Charmaine.

CHARMAINE. What?

VIC. Look at that!

CHARMAINE. What's that?

VIC. 'E's got one of them carpet golf things.

CHARMAINE. Oh, I thought that was a dustpan.

VIC. Don't touch it, it might be a rat-trap!

They both laugh.

VIC. What you do, right? You get a ball (*Demonstrating.*) you knock it in, it shoots out, you knock it in, it shoots out, you knock it in, it shoots out, you knock it in, it shoots out, you knock it in, it shoots out, you knock it in, it shoots out, you knock it in, it shoots out, you knock it in, it shoots out, you knock it in, it shoots out, you knock it in, it shoots out – I saw it on telly – 'ere, don't stand on 'is balls!

They both laugh. VIC belches.

VIC. Oh!

CHARMAINE (*amused*). Oh, 'scuse my pig, 'e's a friend!

VIC. Beg pardon, it's the garlic's comin' back up on me.

CHARMAINE. I'd love a bedroom like this.

VIC. Mind you, it was alright, that turkey rosetti, inasmuch as not likin' it don't apply.

CHARMAINE. I 'ad five 'elpings.

VIC. You never!

CHARMAINE. I did.

VIC. You greedy guts!

CHARMAINE. That's why I stayed in the kitchen: I was blowin' off that much.

They both laugh.

VIC. I like the taste of garlic, but I'm not too keen on the smell; but when it 'its the gastric juices, it comes up in the chest, and you've got to get it up out of the old chimney before it flies out of the back door.

They both laugh.

CHARMAINE. 'Ere, can you smell it on me?

VIC (*smelling*). Nah.

CHARMAINE (*smelling*). I can smell something funny on you.

He smells her; he gives her a subtle kiss; they both laugh.

CHARMAINE. Oh, there's them Spanish dolls!

She goes over to inspect them.

VIC. Yeah: flamingo dancers.

CHARMAINE. Got these great big busts, in they?

VIC. She got any drawers on?

They both laugh.

CHARMAINE. Michelle don't even like garlic.

VIC. Don't she? What'd she put it in for?

CHARMAINE. She was always the one 'oo 'ated spicy foods.

VIC. Did she?

CHARMAINE. Mum says it's Mark's fault.

VIC. Well, Mark's a man of the world, in'e, inasmuch as bubble-and-squeak don't suffice.

CHARMAINE. Look at this bed, Vic: init fabulous?

VIC. Yeah, bleedin' gynormous.

CHARMAINE. 'Ere: what d'you think they wanna big bed like this for?

VIC. It's made to 'er specification, init?

CHARMAINE. What d'you mean?

VIC. So she can 'ave an orgy, inasmuch a gang-bang, while 'e's out and about.

They both laugh. Pause. They stand, looking at the bed.

VIC. 'Ere – shall we give it a try?

CHARMAINE *much amused.*

VIC. Go on – get your coat off!

CHARMAINE *amused.*

VIC (*feeling the bed*). Ooh, it's nice an' 'ard.

CHARMAINE *amused.*

VIC (*sitting*). Ooh, solid as a rock!

CHARMAINE. Get off that bed, Vic!

VIC. Come and sit next to me!

CHARMAINE. You'll leave a big bum-print on it.

They both laugh.

VIC. If I 'ad a place like this, I wouldn't want to go on 'oliday, would you, darlin'?

CHARMAINE. No, I wouldn't.

VIC. Mind you, we're talking about a bloke with a disposable income, inasmuch as 'is pockets is so stuffed up, the grass is greener on the other side inasmuch as 'e's never satisfied.

CHARMAINE. Yeah, well 'e's earned it, though, Vic, en' 'e?

VIC. 'E earns it, I'm not saying 'e don't. Inasmuch as 'e charges 'ere, there an' everywhere like a dog with a banger up 'is arse.

CHARMAINE *laughs.*

VIC. But the question is, 'ow does 'e earn it? Inasmuch as it's immoral earnings.

CHARMAINE. What, are you sayin' 'e's a crook?

VIC. 'E's not a crook, 'e's not a crook as such, inasmuch as 'e don't commit burglary, buggery or butchery; but 'e is inasmuch as 'is morals is all up Shit Creek without a paddle.

CHARMAINE (*sitting*). Yeah; you know when you introduced me to 'im at the firm's 'do' that time?

VIC. Yeah.

CHARMAINE. 'E was very charming an' all that, treated me like I was special; but I thought, slimey!

VIC. You thought right. 'E is slimey . . . inasmuch as 'e nods, smiles, licks their arse and takes their money.

CHARMAINE. 'E's two-faced, in' 'e?

VIC. 'E's like a fork-tongued chameleon. It's a different kettle of fish when I was at the Council, inasmuch the public sector; we was providing a service for the eradication of infestations of vermin of ordinary working citizens.

CHARMAINE. Yeah.

VIC. Inasmuch as it was a vocation more than a chore. Inasmuch as we cared.

CHARMAINE. That's right.

VIC. But with Weasel, inasmuch the private sector, the boot's on the other shoe. 'E's a perpetrator, not an exterminator. Inasmuch as 'e manipulates the public paranoia of the population by stickin' 'is finger in the tub of entomophobic parapsychosis, and givin' it a stir.

CHARMAINE. What's that?

VIC. What's what?

CHARMAINE. That tub o' stuff.

VIC (*looking round*). What tub o' stuff?

CHARMAINE. 'E sticks 'is finger in?

Pause.

VIC. No! Entomophobic parapsychosis!

CHARMAINE. Yeah – what is it?

VIC. The fear of all crawling insects in every man, woman and child.

CHARMAINE. Oh. (*Pause.*) You're not sorry, are you?

VIC. Sorry about what?

CHARMAINE. About leavin' the Council.

VIC. Well, I am inasmuch as I'm a cog in the wheel of Capitalism. Mind you, the extra money comes in 'andy, dunnit?

CHARMAINE. You're telling me. And the free car.

VIC. Yeah. But I've got to put up with it, inasmuch as kow-towing to all 'is foibles and deceits.

CHARMAINE. What d'you mean?

VIC. Take last Tuesday.

CHARMAINE. What?

VIC. 'E bleeps me, I ring 'im back, I say, "Ello Rex, 'ow are you?' 'E says, 'Never mind that – I've got a woman with a spider problem, inasmuch as they're drivin' 'er potty.' I said, 'Rex, spiders is a non-target species, inasmuch as they're of no public health significance; unlike mus musculus, the common 'ouse-mouse, and our old friend rattus rattus.' 'E said, 'Don't give me all that, if she wants to think spiders is a problem, let 'er think spiders is a problem, and it ain't for the likes of you to put 'er on the straight-and-narrow about it, thanking you very much! Get round there, give 'er a good spraying, and eradicate 'em off the face of 'er living-room.' I said, 'I can't do that, Rex: it's against my Code of Ethics.' 'E said, 'Don't you argue the toss with me, do as you're told! Get on your bike, get round there, knock 'em on the 'ead, and charge 'er accordingly.' All 'e cares about is money. 'E's money-mad!

CHARMAINE. I don't blame 'im. I 'ate spiders.

VIC. There's nothing wrong with spiders. Spiders is on our side.
You don't see no flies when there's a spider about – they got
more sense, they keep out of the way! Spiders is the pest-
controllers of the insect world. Ain't no flies on spiders.
Inasmuch the fly, 'e's a disgusting bugger. 'E sits on shit
(CHARMAINE *starts laughing*), shits on it, eats it, flies on your
egg-and-bacon, shits on that, spreads disease and pestilence
all over it, then you eat it.

CHARMAINE's *mirth has taken her to a lying-down position.*

VIC. Oh, look: there's a spider crawling up your leg there.

CHARMAINE (*sitting up*). Where, Vic?!

VIC. There . . .

CHARMAINE *shrieks and giggles as* VIC *runs his finger up her leg
. . . this develops into a gentle, jokey cuddle on the bed. Suddenly,*
CHARMAINE *gets up.*

CHARMAINE. Vic!

VIC. What's up?

CHARMAINE. Someone might 'ear us.

VIC. 'Oo?

CHARMAINE. Upstairs . . .

VIC. Don't worry about that – these places are built like 'Itler's
bleedin' bunker, inasmuch the Reichstag.

CHARMAINE. They wasn't the same thing, Vic.

VIC. Oh, yeah.

CHARMAINE. They might call the police.

VIC. Don't worry about the Old Bill – they're too busy spoiling
people's Christmases.

CHARMAINE. Vic – get off that bed! Look at the state of it!!

She starts straightening the bedding.

VIC. What? 'T's alright – just pull it over!

CHARMAINE. You pull it over!

VIC. Don't fret yourself.

CHARMAINE. 'Ey, Vic.

VIC. What?

CHARMAINE. Does 'e know about you?

VIC. 'Oo?

CHARMAINE. Weasel.

VIC. Know about what?

CHARMAINE. About when you was a kid.

VIC. No, course not! I weren't gonna tell 'im, was I? Wouldn't a got the job. Any'ow, it never came up. Bloke like 'im wouldn't understand. None of 'is business! 'T's all way back in the past, don't count no more. Nobody knows about it. Any'ow, I've 'ad the job for three years now, so it don't apply.

CHARMAINE. Them coppers come round knew about it.

VIC. That's different; they checked the Central Computer, 'cos we was under suspicion.

CHARMAINE. You was under suspicion – I'd been cleared.

VIC. Yeah, well that's the bastard system for you, ain't it, eh? Once they get you on the list, you stay on the list. Don't matter if it's something you did when you was fourteen.

CHARMAINE. Yeah, but you never done it, though, did you?

VIC. But it was me what was sent away, though, wonnit – Muggins?

CHARMAINE. I know, Vic.

VIC. Stays as a black mark against you for the rest of your life. Inasmuch as it's a stigma; I've been stigmatised.

CHARMAINE. Well, I'm sure 'e's got a skeleton in 'is cupboard!

Pause.

VIC. Let's 'ave a look, shall we?

They both laugh. VIC *shines his torch for a few moments at some of the wardrobes; then he creeps up to one, 'Grand Guignol' style, and opens it, mock-surreptitiously.* CHARMAINE, *who has been giggling throughout this, creeps up behind him, and –*

CHARMAINE. Woo!

VIC (*genuinely surprised*). Aaargh!! (*Slams door.*)

CHARMAINE *is convulsed with mirth.*

VIC. Frightened the bleedin' life out of me!

Both laugh; their laughter subsides. CHARMAINE *sits on the dressing-table stool.*

CHARMAINE. Oo, I'm tired, Vic.

VIC *crosses to sit on the blanket-chest.*

VIC. Yeah . . . me an' all.

Pause.

CHARMAINE. Mum's been putting the pressure on Michelle.

VIC. What for?

CHARMAINE. About 'aving a baby.

VIC. Bduh! 'T's bleedin' typical, init?

CHARMAINE. I think Michelle's got her flat too nice, really.

Pause.

VIC. 'Ere: 'oo's to say you ain't gonna be first?

CHARMAINE. I 'ope I will be first, Vic!

VIC. Yeah!

CHARMAINE. I'm getting on.

VIC. Oh, poor old soul!

They both laugh.

VIC. Any'ow, Mark fires blanks, dun 'e?

CHARMAINE. Well, you needn't be so cocky!

They both laugh.

Pause.

VIC. Well . . . we've done our duty; might as well bugger off.

CHARMAINE. Yeah. (*Pause.*) 'Ey, Vic: look at the state of her dressing-table!

VIC. What?

CHARMAINE. Untidy, in't she?

VIC. She's a slut inasmuch as she's untidy in 'er 'abits.

CHARMAINE. Is she?

VIC. It's a well-known fact, inasmuch as she's a bit flighty.

CHARMAINE. 'Oo told you that?

VIC. Leveritt.

CHARMAINE. What'd 'e say?

VIC. 'E told me she was a piss-artist and a slag. Mind you, you can take what 'e says with a pinch of salt, inasmuch as 'e's got something 'orrible to say about everything. 'E wouldn't give you the pickings of 'is nose!

    CHARMAINE *laughs.*

VIC. Mind you, with all that shit, and this flotsam and jetsam, the proof of the pudding's in the eating, init?

    CHARMAINE *offers him a dish of false finger-nails.*

CHARMAINE. 'Ere – d'you want one?

VIC. What's that? (*He takes one.*) Aaargh! Get out of it!! Load of old finger-nails!

CHARMAINE (*amused*). They're only false ones!

VIC. 'Orrible!

CHARMAINE. Vic, I shouldn't 'ave done that!

VIC. You talking about?

CHARMAINE. I've put my fingerprint on it now.

VIC. Don't be daft!

CHARMAINE. 'Ave to clean it off.

VIC. Ain't doin' nothin' criminal.

CHARMAINE (*taking a tissue*). I'll use one o' these.

VIC. We're doing a favour for someone!

CHARMAINE. That's better.

VIC. Oh, look: 'e's got one o' them 'on-suet' bathrooms.

He opens the bathroom door.

CHARMAINE (*looking in the mirror*). Got chocolate on my teeth, Vic.

VIC turns on the bathroom light.

VIC. Cor' – look a' that!

He goes in. CHARMAINE *follows as far as the bathroom doorway.*

CHARMAINE. You're not going to use the library now, are you?

VIC. I'd rather 'ave a shit on me own pot, any day. Oh, look – 'e's got a bidette!

CHARMAINE *has gone in.*

CHARMAINE. Yeh, well 'e needs it, don' 'e?

VIC. She does, you mean.

They both laugh.

VIC. You know what that's for, don't you?

CHARMAINE. Yeah, I know what it's for, Vic.

VIC. Washing your bits out. (*Coming out of the bathroom.*) You get a jet of 'ot water right up your kibosh.

They both laugh.

CHARMAINE (*coming out*). 'E's left 'is toilet-bag be'ind.

VIC. I told you, 'e left in a 'urry. 'T's alright 'avin' one o' them, init, though, eh? Straight out o' bed, on the bog, off the bog, back into bed again! No roaming about in the dark, dark, dank corridor, stubbing your toe an' effin' and blindin'!

CHARMAINE *laughs.*

CHARMAINE. Turn the light off, Vic. Shut the door.

But he was already doing both things in any case.

CHARMAINE. It's a good thing you're wearing them driving-gloves.

VIC. I keep telling you – there's nothing to worry about, inasmuch as it's a good deed well done.

CHARMAINE *is half-way out of the bedroom.*

VIC. Oh look, Charmaine!

CHARMAINE *(coming back).* What?

VIC. Look at that!

CHARMAINE. What's that?

VIC. That thing on the wall. Fire-extinguisher.

CHARMAINE. You gave me a shock, Vic!

VIC. You know what that's for, don't yer?

CHARMAINE. What?

VIC. Smoking in bed.

CHARMAINE *laughs.*

VIC *(doing voice).* 'Oh; oh, oh, darlin', pass me the fire-extinguisher – I'm on fire!'

CHARMAINE. Vic!

VIC. What?

CHARMAINE. You shouldn't say that!

VIC *laughs.*

CHARMAINE. 'Ere – what's she got?

VIC. Load of old pills, inasmuch she must be a junkie, an' all.

They both laugh.

CHARMAINE. Right, Mr Nosey: what's this, then?

VIC. Pot calling the kettle black, init?

CHARMAINE. What is it?

VIC. That's a 'ip-flask.

CHARMAINE. Yeah.

VIC. 'Ere, that's for 'er midnight guzzling.

CHARMAINE. That's right.

VIC. D'you know, I got a call-out once, from this big 'ouse in Golders Green, and there was a woman there 'oo was so alcoholic, she used to 'ave a bottle of cooking-sherry in 'er bedside cabinet. So she could 'ave a swig in the middle o' the night.

CHARMAINE. 'Ow d'you know that?

They are leaving the room.

VIC. 'Er maid told me when she gave me a cuppa tea – 'orrible, it was, tasted like perfume!

He turns off the bedroom light. CHARMAINE *is looking at the shelf-unit. He joins her.*

VIC. Cor'. Look at that lot!

CHARMAINE. Yeah.

VIC. 'T's like a bingo display, init?

CHARMAINE. 'T's not 'omely, is it, Vic?

VIC. Nah; cold.

He turns to another corner of the room.

VIC. Oh, 'ere's all 'is guns! I've used them!

CHARMAINE. What for?

VIC. Pigeon and squirrel killing.

CHARMAINE. Ah!

They disappear towards the front door.

VIC (*off*). You wouldn't want them in your cornflakes, would you? It's all part of the job.

CHARMAINE (*off*). 'Ey, Vic: d'you think I could use the toilet?

VIC (*off*). Yeah – course you can.

CHARMAINE *comes back into the bedroom without putting on the light.*

CHARMAINE. Well I ain't goina do nothing in it.

VIC. What d'you wanna use it for, then?

CHARMAINE *laughs.*

VIC (*off*). I'll 'ave a sit-down.

CHARMAINE (*going to the door*). No, Vic – you come in 'ere with me!

VIC (*off*). Oh, leave off!

CHARMAINE. Come on, Vic: I won't be a minute.

VIC (*off*). Bleedin' 'ell!

He comes in.

CHARMAINE. Better take my coat off.

She does so. VIC *sits on the bed.*

CHARMAINE. Open the door, Vic.

VIC *gets up, goes to the bathroom door, and opens it.*

CHARMAINE. Turn the light on.

He does so. She goes in.

CHARMAINE. Shut the door, Vic.

He does so.

CHARMAINE (*off*). Put yer fingers in yer ears.

VIC. I've 'eard you tinkling 'undreds o' times!

They both laugh.

VIC (*belching*). Oh! (*Another belch.*) Oh! (*Another belch.*) Ah! I'm all stuffed up.

CHARMAINE (*off*). I shouldn't 'ave 'eld on so long.

VIC. I reckon it's the most I've eaten any Christmas all my life. I ain't stopped, 'ave we?

CHARMAINE (*off*). Well, I am definitely going on a diet after this.

VIC. Mind you, that's what it's all about these days, init, Christmas? Stuff it down, stuff it down, stuff it down as much as you can . . . 'T's all about sluff and glotteny. Ain't about the worship and the celebration of the birth of Jesus Christ. Not that I give a gypsy's toss about all that . . . inasmuch as I think it's a load of mumbo-jumbo. Inasmuch as I think it's a load of old bullshit. Mind you . . . the living standards is much 'igher than what it used to be. Notwithstanding 'arf the world's fat, and 'arf the world's dying of starvation. And the other 'arf doesn't know its arse from its elbow. Specially at Christmas- time. There's no rime or reason to it. Plenty o' poor lost souls spending Christmas in a cardboard box, with nothing but a burning piece of plank for a bit o' warmth; nothing but a plastic cup o' soup doled out the back of a van by a patronising God-botherer with nothing better to do on a Christmas night inasmuch as, 'That's yer lot for yer Christmas fare and sustenance!' Mind you; when I was a kid, you was lucky to get so much as an orange and a clip round the ear'ole for Christmas.

CHARMAINE (*off*). I can't wait to get these shoes off – my feet's killing me.

VIC. I did get a kaleidoscope one year. It was bleedin' useless 'cos it was smashed up one end, and all the bits 'ad fallen out. Christmas Day was the only day my ole man didn't knock us about. And that was only in the mornin'! (*Pause.*) What're you doin', 'avin' a bath?

CHARMAINE (*off*). No, but I need one – I smell 'orrible.

VIC. Go on – 'ave one.

They both laugh.

VIC shines his torch on several of the wardrobe doors, making light patterns with the beam. He gets up, goes over to one of the wardrobes, opens it, and has a peep inside. Then he gets in, and closes the door.

By now the toilet has flushed, and CHARMAINE has washed her hands. Pause.

CHARMAINE (*at the door*). Open the door, Vic. (*Pause.*) Vic. (*Pause.*) Vic. (*Pause.*) Vic, open the door!!! VIC!!!

She opens the door herself, and comes out, heading for the other room.

CHARMAINE. Vic!

VIC (*in wardrobe*). Grrrr!!

CHARMAINE. Stop it, Vic!

VIC (*in wardrobe*). Grrrrrr!!

CHARMAINE *picks up her coat.*

CHARMAINE. Vic, stop it!!!! I'm leaving, Vic – I'm goin' now.

VIC bursts out of the wardrobe with a mock-ferocious growl. They both collapse all over the room with uncontrollable mirth.

CHARMAINE. } Ssh! Ssh! Ssh!

VIC.   } Ssh! Ssh!

Their mirth subsides. They embrace in the middle of the room.

VIC. Ah! Ah! Did I frighten it?

Pause. They listen. Voices off.

VIC. D'you 'ear that?

CHARMAINE. Is it next door?

VIC. Sounds like someone's comin' in!

CHARMAINE. D'you think it's burglars?

VIC. Yeah – might be. 'Ide in there! (*He means the wardrobe he's just been in.*)

CHARMAINE. I'm not goin' in there!

VIC. Go on – I'll stand by the door and whack 'em on the 'ead when they come in.

CHARMAINE. Don't be stupid, Vic – you get in with me!

VIC. I'd better 'ad, they might be violent.

   CHARMAINE *gets in the wardrobe, still holding her coat.* VIC *tries to get in with her.*

VIC. I can't get in there – there's no room! I'll get in the next one.

He does so, but gets out again, and rushes to the bathroom to put out the light.

CHARMAINE (*coming out*). Where are you going, Vic?

VIC. I'm turning the light off, shut up! Get in!!

He runs back and gets into his wardrobe again, closing the door. A feather boa is caught outside the door. He pulls this discreetly in.

At this point we again start to register more precisely what we can actually hear. But for practical purposes, here is all that happens offstage, starting just before VIC *says, 'Ah! Ah! Did I frighten it?'*

ROCK *and* MELANIE-JANE *are outside the door of the flat.*

MELANIE-JANE (*off*). My grandma lives in a block of flats. She does. But she only lives on the third floor, so you don't have to use the lift if you don't want to. Is this your front door?

ROCK (*off*). Yeah.

MELANIE-JANE (*off*). Oh, look – there's another front-door. You've got your own front-door keys, haven't you?

ROCK (*off*). Yeah.

MELANIE-JANE (*off*). It's nice, isn't it? 'Cos then you can decide whether you want to come here, or whether you want to go there – whatever you want!

From about here we hear ROCK *and* MELANIE-JANE *more clearly.*

MELANIE-JANE (*off*). They've left the lights on. They have. It's big, isn't it?Shall I close the door? It's bigger from the inside than it is from the outside. I'll close the door.

She closes the door. ROCK *now appears in the bedroom doorway.*

MELANIE-JANE (*off*). I've closed the door!

ROCK *pauses, and puts on the light. Then he comes in, stops, looks at the toys on the floor and around the room in general, and goes and sits on the bed.*

Throughout this, MELANIE-JANE *has continued regardless . . .*

MELANIE-JANE (*off*). Oh, what's that? I haven't seen one of those before! Is this where you have your dinner parties? I like this flat, it's gorgeous. There's a horrible ugly bull on top of that bookshelf. There is.

She comes into view through the doorway.

I went to a bullfight when I was in Barcelona with my Daddy. It gave me a toothache. What are you doing? You've got some guns. You have. Why have you got these guns? I don't like guns.

Pause. She is in the doorway.

(*Giggling.*) This is a big bedroom, isn't it? Is this your bedroom? (*Pause.*) Is it, Rocky?

Pause.

ROCK. No.

Pause.

MELANIE-JANE. It's your Mummy and Daddy's bedroom, isn't it?

Pause.

ROCK. Yeah.

Pause.

MELANIE-JANE (*giggling*). Oh, dear! Who do those toys belong to?

Pause.

ROCK. They're my Mum's.

MELANIE-JANE. Is that your Daddy's exercise-bike?

ROCK. No, it's my Mum's.

MELANIE-JANE (*giggling*). Are we allowed to be in here? We're not, are we?

Pause.

ROCK. Yeah.

Pause.

MELANIE-JANE. I'm not allowed in my Mummy and Daddy's bedroom. I'm not. Oh, yes I was, on my twenty-first birthday! People were allowed to put their coats on the bed. Well, it wasn't actually on my birthday, it was at my party. 'Cos my birthday was on the Thursday, and my party was on the Saturday. We were going to have my party on the Thursday, but I work late on a Thursday. Well, I did that Thursday, anyway. So we decided to have it on the Saturday, so that people could sleep late on the Sunday. (*Giggles.*) But you know – you were there, weren't you? (*Giggles.*) Did you put your coat on my Mummy and Daddy's bed?

Pause.

ROCK. No.

Pause.

MELANIE-JANE. Where's your bedroom?

Pause.

ROCK. I don't live here, do I?

MELANIE-JANE. No, I know you don't live here now; but what d'you do when you come to visit?

ROCK. There isn't another bedroom. This is the only one.

MELANIE-JANE. Where do you sleep, then?

Pause.

ROCK. My Dad doesn't want me here.

MELANIE-JANE. Doesn't he? (*Giggles.*) That's not very nice, is it? My Daddy likes me living at home. He does. I think he does anyway. I need to go to the toilet . . . Can I use the toilet, please? Where's the bathroom?

Pause.

(*Giggling.*) Where is it?

Pause.

ROCK (*gesturing vaguely*). It's over there.

MELANIE-JANE. Oh, yes. I didn't see it. I should've gone in the pub, but I don't like that toilet very much. (*Looking in.*) You've got a bidet! My Mummy wants a bidet. My Mummy's agoraphobic. Daddy won't let her have one, though. (*Going in.*) Oh, (*Giggling.*) you can see yourself when you're sitting on the toilet! Where's the light switch? – Oh, there it is! (*Turns on the light.*) I won't be a minute. (*Closes the door. Giggling.*) I can see you through the door. I can. Can you see me?

Pause. Opens the door.

ROCK. Yeah.

MELANIE-JANE. Don't you want to go into the living-room? Watch the television? The film? (*Pause. Giggles.*) You'll have to go out. You will. I don't think I can do it if you're sitting there. (*Pause.*) Please, Rocky . . .

Pause. Then she runs over to him, takes him by the hands, and tries to pull him up.

MELANIE-JANE. Come on – don't be a silly sausage! I'll have an accident, and then you'll get into trouble with your Mummy and Daddy. Please, Rocky – don't be a spoilsport. (*He allows her to pull him up.*) That's right, there's a good boy. In here.

(*She pushes him into the living-room. Off.*) You sit down there, and get comfortable. (*She comes back into the bedroom.*) I won't be long! (*She goes into the bathroom, and closes the door.*)

Pause: nothing happens on stage. Then ROCK *enters, now wearing his earphones. His Walkman is on – loud enough for the heavy beat of the music to be audible. He holds the packet of cooking-chocolate, and is eating some. He walks round the bed, and stands looking at it for a while, near the bathroom door.*

The toilet is flushed. Pause. MELANIE-JANE *opens the door. On seeing* ROCK, *she stops in her tracks. Pause. She turns off the bathroom light. They look at each other. Pause. Then she runs across the room to the door. Pause. She goes out, and immediately re-enters.*

MELANIE-JANE. Aren't we going to sit on the sofa? I think I'll just take my coat off.

She goes out. ROCK *moves as if to come round the bed and follow her, but instead stops and sits on the end of the bed. His tape is still audible.*

MELANIE-JANE (*off*). Can I have a look at some of your records? (*Pause.*) Liberace! You've got Liberace. (*She appears in the doorway, holding a Liberace album; she has taken off her coat and her glasses.*) He's my Mummy's favourite. (ROCK *turns off the tape, and takes off his cans.*) She used to play him all the time at home; and then he died; and now Daddy doesn't let her play him any more. (*Pause.*) Oh, look at those trophies! (*She goes out to them, remaining in view.*) My Daddy plays golf. He does. I used to wait for him in the car while he practised at this special place; all you could see was the golf-balls flying through the air . . . you couldn't see who was hitting them, though.

ROCK. There's over two million prostitutes in Thailand.

Pause.

MELANIE-JANE. Shall we sit in there?

ROCK. My Dad used to make me carry his golf-clubs.

MELANIE-JANE. My brother used to carry my Daddy's golf-clubs. He got five pounds a week pocket-money for it.

ROCK. Did he? You wouldn't catch my Dad giving me anything. You know when I was working at Pizza-Pronto? I was only earning seventy pounds a week, and he wanted me to give him fifty!

MELANIE-JANE. Did he?

ROCK. Yeah. (*Pause.*) That was when I left college. It wasn't my fault I didn't get my 'A' Levels.

MELANIE-JANE. 'A' Levels are horrible.

ROCK. That would have only left me twenty pounds a week to buy all my clothes with. (*Pause.*) Anyway, he doesn't need the money – he's practically a millionaire. He's a bloody sadist. He locked me out of the house. He got me this bedsit without even telling me – he moved all my stuff in there.

MELANIE-JANE. Did he?

ROCK. Even my stereo. I wasn't going to live there. I had to stay with a mate. I never gave him the money, though. I went back home, and all my stuff was there. He never said anything.

MELANIE-JANE. Didn't he?

ROCK. No. I woke up on the Saturday, though, and there was an estate agent in my bedroom, measuring everything.

MELANIE-JANE (*sitting on the bed, not next to him*). Your Daddy let an estate agent in your bedroom? Did he?

ROCK. He put the house up for sale. He didn't even tell my Mum.

MELANIE-JANE. My Daddy wouldn't let an estate agent in my bedroom. He wouldn't

ROCK. Then he went and bought this place.

Pause.

MELANIE-JANE. This is a hard bed, isn't it?

Long pause.

ROCK. My Dad's a wanker.

Long pause.

MELANIE-JANE. Are you going to stay here tonight? (*Long pause.*) Or are you going back to Chris's? (*Long pause.*) Which?

Pause. MELANIE-JANE *sits next to* ROCK.

Can I have some of your chocolate? Can I? What have you
got? It's cooking chocolate! You're eating cooking chocolate.
You are. My Daddy might have to go to Sweden on business.
He had to 'phone them yesterday. He's been there before,
though. He had to go to the office. He was there all
afternoon. Fancy having to work on Boxing Day! Mummy
wouldn't speak to anybody. I'll just have a little piece. (*She
takes some chocolate, and puts the packet on the bed beside her.*) D'you
know what I did on Christmas Day? I had to lay the dinner
table, and I put the forks where the knives were meant to be,
and the knives where the forks were meant to be. (*Giggles.*)
Aren't I silly? Daddy hit me on the back of the head . . . with
a cork table-mat . . . I've still got the bump; I play with it in
bed. D'you want to feel it? (*She offers it to* ROCK*; he doesn't
react.*) He was only joking though. (*Pause.*) These table-mats
have scenes on them, of Stratford-upon-Avon. They have.
And this one has Anne Hathaway's cottage on it, with a little
picture in the corner of Lady Macbeth with her daggers.
(*Pause.*) Does your Mummy dye her hair?

ROCK *kisses* MELANIE-JANE, *quickly and suddenly. At first, she
responds; then she jumps away from him.*

You taste of chocolate! – Oh dear, I'm sitting on it! (*Pause.
Then she takes off a shoe.*) My shoes need re-heeling. I don't
wear these to work, though, 'cos they're too high. Oh, look –
there's Kermit the Frog. (*She joins Kermit on the floor.*) Hello,
Kermit the Frog! (*Doing voice.*) 'Hello, Melanie-Jane' (*Giggles.*) I
used to have a Kermit the Frog puppet. I did. I used to stick
my hand up his bottom to make his mouth move.

Pause.

ROCK. I saw Keith Chegwyn the other day in W. H. Smith's.

MELANIE-JANE. Did you? What was he doing?

Pause.

ROCK. I dunno. Buying something.

MELANIE-JANE. Perhaps he was doing his last-minute Christmas
shopping. What's that? Oh, it's a mouse!

ROCK *goes to the dressing-table.*

MELANIE-JANE. I've still got three teddy-bears at home. I have.
D'you know what I call them? I call them Teddy-Bear 1,

Teddy-Bear 2 and Teddy-Bear 3. Teddy-Bear 3's my
favourite. I let him sleep with me in my bed. I've got a single
bed. I haven't got a double bed. I've never slept in a double
bed . . . well, not properly . . .

*ROCK has picked up a perfume-spray; he gives it a brief,
unexpressive squirt. Pause.*

What're you doing? (*Pause. He looks at her. Then another squirt/*)
Is that your Mummy's perfume? (*Another squirt.*) Are you
spraying your Mummy's perfume? (*Another squirt. She goes
towards him.*) Don't . . . you'll get it on the carpet. Mm – that's
a nice smell, isn't it? (*He sprays her.*) Don't spray me! (*He sprays
her again; she runs away.*) Don't! (*Returning.*) I want a go! (*Spray.*)
Rocky! Give it to me! (*Spray.*) Help!!! (*She runs away again.*) I'm
going to put my shoe on. You're not allowed to spray me
until I've got my shoe on. Pax! (*Holding up one hand, crossing her
fingers. She stands on one foot in order to put her other shoe on. He
sprays her. She falls over, giggling hysterically.*) That's not fair –
that's cheating! I'm going to get Kermit the Frog to protect
me. (*She picks up Kermit, and holds him out in front of her.*) You've
got to give it to us now. (*He sprays them. She puts Kermit behind
her with his arms around her waist.*) You're not allowed to spray
Kermit! Give it to me! I want it now! You've got to give it to
me! (*Struggling with* ROCK.) Rocky! Let me have it! (*She falls
onto the bed, with a bit of help from* ROCK. *She lies there, giggling.
Pause.*) That's not fair. That's not supposed to happen. (*Getting
up.*) I'll just put it back. Where does it go? Oh, yes. (*She puts
the perfume-bottle back. To Kermit.*) You sit there. (*Sits Kermit on
the stool; as an afterthought she crosses his legs. Pause. She is still
giggling.* ROCK *and* MELANIE-JANE *are standing close to each
other.*) That was a good game, wasn't it? (*He kisses her. Again she
responds at first for a moment, then pushes him off.*) You are funny!
(*She runs across the room.*) I think I'll have a cigarette . . . I'll
just go and get one.

Exit MELANIE-JANE. ROCK *hovers by the bed.*

MELANIE-JANE (*off*). Can I have a cup of tea?

She comes back with a cigarette and a large, expensive table-lighter.

This is nice, isn't it? My Daddy sells these. He sells
computers, as well. (*She lights the cigarette;* ROCK *takes out a
handkerchief, and blows his nose.*) I'll just put it back.

Exit MELANIE-JANE. ROCK *takes off his jacket and moves to the head of the bed on the bathroom side. He takes the cassette out of his Walkman, and puts it in the radio/cassette player by the bed.*

MELANIE-JANE *appears in the doorway. She is wearing her glasses.*

Ooh, dear. I'd better not smoke in here. (*Tries to disperse the smoke.*) We had ham at Christmas as well as turkey, because Grandma Beetles doesn't like turkey; she says it reminds her of Grandpa Beetles. (*Pause. The music – Madonna – has started.*) Does Madonna *know* Michael Jackson . . . d'you think . . . ?

Pause.

ROCK. I dunno.

MELANIE-JANE. I need an ashtray. (*Sees one by the bed.*) Oh. I wish my Mummy and Daddy smoked.

She sits on the bed. They are now both sitting on the bed, one on each side. Pause.

ROCK. Jogging causes depression.

MELANIE-JANE. Does it? Oh, dear!

ROCK. People who jog a lot get jogger's nipple.

MELANIE-JANE. What's jogger's nipple?

Pause.

ROCK. Dunno.

Pause.

MELANIE-JANE. Sounds like an ice-cream. (*Pause.*) Did you try my socks on?

ROCK. No.

MELANIE-JANE. Don't you like them?

ROCK (*no response.*)

MELANIE-JANE. I got all my Christmas presents from work this year. I did. 'Cos you get discount. D'you get discount at your shoe-shop?

Pause.

ROCK. Yeah.

MELANIE-JANE. Did you buy anybody any shoes for Christmas?

ROCK. No.

MELANIE-JANE. No . . . I didn't get anybody any toys. (*Pause.*)
    I'm not looking forward to the January sales . . . it's not fair.
    Oh, dear! – I'd better not get ash on the bed . . . keep it nice
    and clean or your Daddy will be cross.

ROCK. My Dad has the whole flat sprayed each month.

MELANIE-JANE. Does he? What with?

    Pause.

ROCK. A spray.

MELANIE-JANE. One of those air-fresheners? We're not allowed
    to have those in our house. We're not. 'Cos Mummy's
    allergic to them. Daddy says the house smells like a Chinese
    brothel on Confucius's birthday. He does – he always says
    that! (*Giggles.*)

ROCK. It's insecticide.

    Pause.

MELANIE-JANE. What's insecticide?

ROCK. What they spray.

MELANIE-JANE. Ergh! Yukkie!

ROCK. When we lived in Tudor Road, they used to get me out of
    bed so they could spray my bedroom.

MELANIE-JANE. Who used to get you out of bed?

ROCK. My Dad. His men used to come round with a spray-gun.
    He was always getting them round. He makes them do things
    for him.

MELANIE-JANE. What sort of things?

ROCK. They have to put up fences; mend the toilet; drive him
    about . . . They even had to pick up my Mum once when she
    broke down on the North Circular. She was wearing a bikini.
    (*Pause.*) He thinks he's still in the Army.

MELANIE-JANE. My brother was in the Army. He was. The
    King's Troop Royal Horse Artillery. He's not any more,
    though. He sells computers. He rode his horse at Lord

Mountbatten's funeral. He did. We watched him on the television – it was really funny. He was hoping to be at the Queen Mother's funeral before he left. He was really disappointed. They have special black horses just to pull the coffins . . . (*Pause.*) Do the men have to spray this bed? Do they? There was a spider in my wardrobe last summer; there was; it was Daddy's birthday . . . I bought him a bull-worker . . . he was really cross. It was one of those whitey spiders – well, sort of grey. I opened the door, and it just disappeared! It ran into one of my shoes; I didn't know which one, so I waited for it to come out . . . but it didn't. I stood there for ages. In the end I just closed the door and went downstairs. Everybody was waiting for me. (*Pause.*) Have you ever seen a cockroach?

ROCK (*no response*).

MELANIE-JANE *moves to face* ROCK *directly, at close quarters, kneeling.*

MELANIE-JANE. When I was seven I had all my hair cut off. I did, 'cos I had lice. It wasn't very nice. I couldn't stop scratching for ages. I kept thinking they were going to crawl down my face and get into my head through my mouth, or through my ears, or up my nose . . . and eat my eyeballs from behind, and have my brains for breakfast.

ROCK *embraces and kisses her again; they roll over on the bed; for a few moments* MELANIE-JANE *responds, making furtive clutching movements, scratching* ROCK's *back with small gestures. Then she suddenly withdraws, and sits up abruptly.*

Be careful of my glasses, Rocky! I don't want to break them again. They're very exclusive frames.

MELANIE-JANE *gets up.* ROCK *stays on the bed.* MELANIE-JANE *starts moving around the room. The following should be slightly frenetic.*

D'you think I should get contact lenses? Daddy thinks I should get coloured ones. Mummy doesn't, though; she says my eyes are a nice colour the way they are. I'm going to have a go on this. (*She mounts the exercise-bike, but she doesn't pedal.*) D'you know what the time is? I'll have to be getting a taxi soon. (*She gets off the bike, and goes to the dressing-table.*) We had a nice time this evening, didn't we? Look at my hair. (*Going towards the door.*) Do you have a taxi number? (*Exits.*) I wonder what time it is. (*Enters.*) Have you ever played 'Trivial Pursuits'? OH, LOOK: THERE'S AN ALBATROSS!!! (*Big burst of giggles. She sits on the blanket chest and examines her hair.*) I've got a lot of split ends. (*Opens and closes the blanket chest.*) Oh, it's like a coffin. (*Crosses the room.*) We'll see each other in the week, though, won't we, Rocky? I like the sausages with the herbs in them best. (*Touching the wardrobes containing* VIC *and* CHARMAINE.) Your Mummy and Daddy must have a lot of clothes. (*Moves away from these wardrobes, and opens and closes a nearby one. Pause.*) We've known each other for a long time, haven't we, Rocky? Since when we were at college together. Can I have a little peep? (*She opens and closes yet another wardrobe, then moves back towards* VIC *and* CHARMAINE's *two, stopping at the next one along, which she opens and closes. Pause.*) Do you like me, Rocky?

ROCK. *No response. Long pause.*

MELANIE-JANE *goes to* CHARMAINE's *wardrobe.*

MELANIE-JANE. I think I'll have a look in this one. (*Tries it.* CHARMAINE *is holding it closed from inside.*) Oh – it's locked!

She opens the next one, and sees VIC. *She slams it shut, screaming; she bolts across the room.*

MELANIE-JANE. THERE'S A MAN IN THAT CUPBOARD!!!!!

ROCK *stares at her.*

THERE IS!!! (*She is extremely distraught.*)

THERE'S A MAN IN THERE!!!!

She takes a pillow from the bed, and hugs it.

ROCKY!! THERE'S A MAN IN THE CUPBOARD!!!

Crying, agitated, unhinged, terrified.

ROCKY!!!!

Long pause, during which she becomes increasingly upset.

I DON'T LIKE THIS GAME!!!!!

She rushes into the toilet, and locks the door.

Very long pause. MELANIE-JANE's *crying dies down, first to a whimper, and then to silence.* ROCK *is baffled and immobile.*

Eventually VIC's *door opens slowly, and he emerges from the darkness and from Mrs Weasel's gaudy collection, still holding his torch . . .*

VIC. Good evening, Master Weasel . . . inasmuch I presume you're Master Weasel . . . (*He closes the door.*) Er . . . my name is Mr Maggott; inasmuch Victor Maggott . . .

CHARMAINE *opens her door, and begins to emerge. She is still holding her coat.*

VIC. This is my wife, Mrs Maggott . . . she, er . . .

CHARMAINE *holds up her coat, as though to protect herself from seeing the unseeable. She runs across and out of the room;* VIC *follows her . . .*

VIC. Charmaine! Charmaine! (*Stopping in the doorway.*) Everything ain't what it looks like . . . inasmuch what you're seeing . . . ain't what it seems; d'you get what I'm saying? What I'm saying . . . is that I've been requested, as it were. . . to give the place the once-over, inasmuch check it out . . . and make sure that everything is shipshape and Bristol-fashion.

CHARMAINE (*off.*) We never touched nothin'!!!

VIC. No, that's right, we ain't – only door-fastenings and window-casements; and I can safely report that there is no visible sign of breaking-and-entering, inasmuch skulduggery and other various felonies.

CHARMAINE (*appearing*). Anyway, my husband's been wearin' 'is driving gloves.

VIC. That's right: a Christmas present from my good lady wife here. A very practical gift indeed. Only we was led to believe that the flat was empty, inasmuch as your mother and father were on their Christmas vacation inasmuch as there was no-one 'ere.

CHARMAINE. That was what we was told, anyway, wanit, Vic?

VIC. We was on our way 'ome inasmuch as we don't actually live in this vicinity.

CHARMAINE. No, we live in North London.

VIC. Inasmuch the London Borough of Islin'ton.

CHARMAINE. That's right.

VIC. D'you know it, by any chance?

CHARMAINE. No, 'e won't know it, Vic.

VIC. 'E might . . . It's got two prisons.

CHARMAINE. My sister always 'as us down after Christmas.

VIC. We was killing one bird with two stones.

CHARMAINE. We all go round to my Mum's on Christmas Day, don't we, Vic?

VIC. Wouldn't miss it for the world!

CHARMAINE. Her 'usband works for Britannia Airways.

VIC. Check-in.

CHARMAINE. They live just round the corner from 'ere – Thamesmeade Court: d'you know it?

VIC. Nice flats, private.

CHARMAINE. She give us a lovely evening, dint she, Vic?

VIC. She always does us proud.

CHARMAINE. She's very generous, my sister, in't she, Vic?

VIC. Very generous!

CHARMAINE. Anyway, you was just doin' someone a favour, wun' you, Vic?

VIC. That's right!

CHARMAINE. Mr Stoat.

VIC. That's right – Roy Stoat. You know Roy Stoat, don't you? – your father's second-in-command. A decent sort . . .

CHARMAINE. I told you we shouldn't 'ave said yes.

VIC. 'E's only shown me nothing but friendship and kindness, inasmuch as one good deed deserves another!

CHARMAINE. 'E's too good-natured, my 'usband – I'm always telling 'im that!

VIC. Don't be daft, darlin'. (*Pause.*) What it is . . . what it is, you see, inasmuch . . . is that 'e's been obligated; 'e's 'ad to go to Uttoxeter to visit 'is in-laws; but between me, you and the gate-post, inasmuch within these three walls, 'e's doin' a bit o' moonlighting on the Q.T. . . . 'cos 'e's supposed to be on call over the Christmas Season, keeping people's festive tables free from unwanted visitors, notwithstanding a favour pledged to your father to stick 'is mush in this place and give it a quick shufti to alleviate 'is worries and vexations; but what with 'is own domestic ramifications, 'e's asked me to do the favour for 'im . . . ain' 'e?

CHARMAINE. Yeah . . .

VIC. Inasmuch . . . in lieu . . .

CHARMAINE. 'E come round to us with the keys . . . last Wednesday, wunit, Vic?

VIC. That's right.

CHARMAINE. Day before Christmas Eve. And I offered 'im a cup of tea . . .

VIC. It was too early for alcoholic beverages, notwithstanding the time of year.

CHARMAINE. But 'e didn't want one, 'cos 'is wife and kids was downstairs in the car with the luggage . . .

VIC. They was worried about finding the M1.

CHARMAINE. We're five floors up.

VIC. You know Roy Stoat, don't yer?

ROCK (*no response*).

VIC. Big, tall, skinny fellow with a skull face; looks like an American, wears a baseball 'at. Comes from Morden.

CHARMAINE. Talks real quiet . . .

Pause.

VIC. I'd've thought you'd 'ave known 'im.

Pause.

ROCK. I do know 'im.

CHARMAINE. There you are, Vic.

VIC. Well, that's 'im!!!!

Pause.

ROCK. D'you work for my Dad?

CHARMAINE. Yes, 'e does!

VIC. 'Course I do, I've worked for your father for nigh on three years, all but a few months, inasmuch as I've never 'ad a day off!

CHARMAINE. Except for 'is Grandad's funeral.

VIC. Yeah, but that weren't with bad 'ealth!

CHARMAINE. No!

VIC. 'E's my boss. I work for 'im . . . and I'm doin' a favour for 'im but 'e don't know 'e's 'avin' a favour done for . . .

CHARMAINE. Yeah, cos your Dad's in Spain with your Mum, ain' 'e?

Pause.

ROCK. No.

VIC. Ain't 'e?

Pause.

ROCK. No. (*Pause.*) They're not in Spain.

Pause.

VIC. Oh, that's right – 'e's in Tenerife, ain't they?

ROCK. No.

VIC. Ain't they?

ROCK. No.

VIC. Where are they, then?

Pause.

ROCK. They're in Lanzarote.

VIC. Well, it's the same thing, init?

Pause.

ROCK. No.

VIC. Yes, it is.

ROCK. No, it's not.

VIC. 'Course it is! 'T's the Canary Islands, init? Lanzarote, Gran

Canaria, Tenerife! Inasmuch Lanzarote is a volcano, and it rose out of the sea, and all of its sand is volcanic ash and therefore bleedin' useless for making sandcastles.

But ROCK *is inspecting* VIC's *wardrobe.*

ROCK. Yeah, but they're not in Tenerife.

VIC. It's alright – there's nobody else in there.

CHARMAINE. Vic – the keys. You've got the keys!!

VIC. Oh, yeah! Roy give me the keys, didn' 'e? 'Ere y'are: two Yale, one Chubb! 'Ere, why don't you check my pockets while you're about it?

CHARMAINE. You can look in my bag, if you like.

VIC. Yeah, 'ave a look in 'er bag – look, nothing!

CHARMAINE (*looking in her bag*). Well, I do admit I did borrow one of your Mum's tissues.

VIC. It's alright, I can pay for that, I've got money. (*Jingles his pocket.*)

ROCK *is now inspecting* CHARMAINE's *wardrobe.*

CHARMAINE. Everything's just as it was in there.

VIC. She wouldn't touch nothing that weren't 'ers.

CHARMAINE. You can ask my sister – we told 'er we was coming 'ere on the way 'ome, didn't we, Vic?

VIC. That's right!

CHARMAINE. Phone 'er and check, if you like.

VIC. Yeah – go on, give 'er a call!

CHARMAINE. The car, Vic!!

VIC. What?

CHARMAINE. Downstairs!

VIC. Oh yeah, course: me car! You know the firm's cars don't yer? White Ford Fiestas with the name down the side: 'Vermination. The Pest Patrol.'

CHARMAINE. Why don't you come and 'ave a look?

VIC. Yeah – didn't you see it parked downstairs in front of that smashed-up Jag?

CHARMAINE. It's got all 'is stuff in it, enit, Vic?

VIC. That's right, inasmuch all the tools of my trade. You've got yer bait-boxes, you've got yer sticky-boards, you got yer Brodifacoum, yer Villsen Pyramids, you've got yer insecticide – I've even got a brand-new Insectocutor, ready for installation, 'aven't I, Charmaine?

CHARMAINE. Yeah – it's like a walking death-trap in there – I can 'ardly get in.

VIC. Would you care to accompany me to the vehicle, then? Inasmuch see 'oo I am, what I'm talking about? Your wish is our demand, young Mr Weasel.

ROCK *has now inspected two more wardrobes, and is on to his fifth; he ignores* VIC *and* CHARMAINE.

VIC. I don't know what else to say to convince you . . .

CHARMAINE. I 'ope your girlfriend ain't poorly.

ROCK *goes and has a look through the bathroom door.*

VIC. Yeah – shock can give you the collywobbles . . .

CHARMAINE. Yeah . . .

VIC. Inasmuch the gyp.

CHARMAINE *advances towards* ROCK, *who remains with his back to them.*

CHARMAINE. I'm sorry we spoiled things for you.

ROCK (*no response*).

CHARMAINE. 'Scuse me . . .

Pause. MELANIE-JANE *is moving towards the door.*

CHARMAINE. Oh, I think she's comin' out!

Pause. MELANIE-JANE *opens the door, and comes out, holding the pillow.*

CHARMAINE. Ah, 'ere she is!

VIC. Eh . . . she's as right as ninepence, ain't she?

CHARMAINE. Yeah, she is. 'Ow are you now, love? (*To* ROCK.) You should get 'er a brandy.

VIC *assumes a bizarre posture.*

VIC. See! I ain't the bogeyman!

VIC *and* CHARMAINE *laugh hugely.*

CHARMAINE. D'you know, I've been married to him for six years, and I still get a fright when I look at him!

VIC. Shut up! Giz a kiss!!

VIC *and* CHARMAINE *laugh some more.*

ROCK. Are you gonna tell my Dad?

VIC. What?

ROCK. That you saw us here.

VIC. No, course not! We wouldn't do a thing like that – would we, Charmaine?

MELANIE-JANE. Why, aren't we allowed to be here, then?

ROCK. Yeah.

VIC. It's none of our business, is it? Inasmuch as it's your alienable prerogative to be in this residence, inasmuch as you're a member of the Weasel family, inasmuch as it's your God-given right!

MELANIE-JANE. Are we?

CHARMAINE. Anyway, we was just as scared as you was.

VIC. We thought you was intruders.

CHARMAINE. Yeah, I thought my end had come!

VIC. You was lucky I didn't give you a whack on the nut.

CHARMAINE. And when you was talking about spiders, I could feel them crawling all over me!

VIC *and* CHARMAINE *laugh uproariously, whilst* ROCK *crosses, and inspects the last remaining wardrobe not containing* REX; VIC *and* CHARMAINE *join him and have a look.*

VIC. Nothing.

CHARMAINE. No.

Long pause, during which CHARMAINE *silently but expressively communicates sympathy to* MELANIE-JANE, *e.g. miming 'Are you alright?', shuddering at shared horrors of spiders and bogeymen in cupboards, raising eyes heavenwards about the men, etc.*

VIC. Well . . . this ain't going to get the pig a new bonnet, is it?

CHARMAINE. No.

VIC. Inasmuch time's getting on, and these two young people want to get to their bed.

VIC and CHARMAINE *laugh uproariously.* ROCK *moves towards the last* (REX's) *wardrobe, but –*

VIC. Right, then: if everything's alright with you, we'll be taking our leave, eh, Charmaine?

CHARMAINE. Yeah.

VIC. Would you by any chance 'ave such a thing as a pencil and a piece of paper?

ROCK. There's a message-pad by the fridge.

VIC. Good! 'Cos what I'm going to do for you is, I'm going to log my credentials, inasmuch give you my name, address, telephone number and postal code . . .

CHARMAINE. That's a good idea, Vic.

VIC. And should anything untoward arise from our untimely visitation, do not 'esitate to contact me, inasmuch let me know.

ROCK, VIC *and* CHARMAINE *have filed out of the room, followed after a moment by* MELANIE-JANE, *who now stands alone in the doorway, still holding the pillow.* CHARMAINE *reappears.*

CHARMAINE. It was nice meeting you.

MELANIE-JANE. It was very nice to meet you, as well.

VIC (*off*). Oh, good – a detachable pad.

MELANIE-JANE. Bye bye!

CHARMAINE. 'Bye.

CHARMAINE returns to the others in the kitchen. MELANIE-JANE *comes back into the room; she replaces the pillow, sits on the bed, and proceeds to put on her shoes.*

VIC (*off*). Now what I'm gonna do is to write my name and address on 'ere and give it to you . . . and I want you to fold it neatly, and put it in yer inside pocket, and nobody need know about it . . . alright?

MELANIE-JANE has got her shoes on, and is quietly recomposing herself.

VIC (*off*). Right. Now . . . we are Mr . . . and Mrs . . . Victor . . . Maggott . . . and we live at seventy-four –

REX pops his head round the wardrobe door, thinking the room is empty. He is still holding the gun.

MELANIE-JANE (*screaming and running across the room*). NO!!! NO!!!!

REX immediately withdraws into the wardrobe, and closes the door. MELANIE-JANE is further confused and hysterical.

CHARMAINE rushes in, followed by VIC.

CHARMAINE. } What's the matter? Wait a minute!
VIC.　　　 } What's 'appening?

MELANIE-JANE, now very fraught, starts throwing stuffed animals at REX's wardrobe; some of these go in CHARMAINE's direction, possibly hitting her. CHARMAINE and VIC rush out, closing the door. REX comes out of the wardrobe.

REX. Alright, calm down! (*MELANIE-JANE runs towards the bathroom.*) Stand still! – No, don't go in there! (*She goes in.*) I want to go in there – I want to use it!!! (*She has locked the door; REX has rushed across to stop her, but he is too late.*) Come out, you stupid girl!!! COME OUT!!!!

VIC has crept back into the room, unseen by REX, at whom he now stands gaping. REX stops, turns round, and stares back at VIC. Pause.

VIC. Fuck my old boots!!!!

Exit VIC, followed by REX.

REX. Maggott!! Maggott!!! MAGGOTT!!!!

Blackout

ACT TWO

The same, a few moments later. ROCK *is outside the bathroom, facing* REX. REX *is very tense. He is pointing the gun at* ROCK.

REX. Talk to 'er! Go on! She's your bloody girlfriend – tell 'er! She's in my bathroom! What are you waiting for? Don't just stand there!

Pause.

Look at you! You pillock! You great streak of yellow piss! You're bloody useless!!

VIC *appears at the door, with* CHARMAINE *behind him.*

VIC. 'Scuse me, boss . . .

REX. What do you want, Maggott?

VIC. Er –

REX. Wh?

VIC. You are 'ere, then?

REX. What?!

VIC. Inasmuch you ain't an apparatition, inasmuch you ain't been beamed down from another planet?

CHARMAINE *giggles.*

VIC. – Shut up, Charmaine – inasmuch as I ain't goin' round the bend and you're 'ere in your flat in your lovely bedroom 'ere?

REX. Yes, I'm here alright, Maggott – large as bloody life!

REX *waves the gun at* VIC, *and goes over to the bathroom.*

VIC. Alright, boss!

Pause.

REX. Right! Maggott: come 'ere!!

VIC. What?

REX. Sit on the bed!

VIC. I beg your pardon?

REX. And your lady wife!

VIC. What, on the bed?

REX. You heard me – come on!

VIC. What for?

REX. 'Cos I say so – COME ON!!!

VIC. Alright, Rex – anything you want. I can explain everything.

REX. Oh, can you?

VIC. Yeah. Come on, darlin'.

> CHARMAINE *sits on the bed.*

CHARMAINE. D'you 'ave a nice Christmas, Mr Weasel?

REX (*going towards the door*). Bloody awful, thank you!

VIC. Go easy with the blunderbuss there, boss!

REX. Shut up. And don't move.

> *He goes and shuts the door. Pause.*

CHARMAINE (*getting up*). What's 'e up to?

VIC. I dunno. (*Belches.*)

CHARMAINE. Vic!

VIC. That's shock, that is.

CHARMAINE. Are you alright?

VIC. Yeah. (*Pause.*) Where'd 'e bleedin' pop up from?

CHARMAINE. 'E must 'ave come in through the front door.

VIC. When?

CHARMAINE. When we was in the kitchen.

VIC. No, 'e never.

CHARMAINE (*to* ROCK). Didn't 'e?

VIC (*to* ROCK). Did 'e?

ROCK (*no response*).

VIC. You was facing that way! D'you see 'im?

CHARMAINE. I don't think 'e did, Vic.

VIC. Course not.

CHARMAINE. What's she up to?

VIC. Eh? (*Pause*.) Oi!

CHARMAINE. What?

VIC. 'E was already in 'ere, wan' 'e?

CHARMAINE. Don't be so daft, Vic – where?

VIC. I dunno. (*Inspecting the bed*.) No – it's a divan.

   Pause.

CHARMAINE. We'll be lucky to get out of 'ere alive!

VIC. Oh, don't worry about that.

CHARMAINE. Don't tell me not to worry, Vic – I'm scared stiff of that thing!

VIC. 'E's playin' cops-and-robbers – it's only an airgun; it can't kill yer – it'll just give yer a nasty sting up yer bum.

CHARMAINE. I 'ope you're right.

VIC. Course I'm right. That thing's too small.

CHARMAINE. What thing?

VIC. That hottoman. (*He is referring to the blanket chest*.)

CHARMAINE. Yeah, it is. (*Giggles*.)

VIC. There's nowhere else *to* 'ide.

CHARMAINE. Only the cupboards.

VIC. Don't be ridiculous!

   They both laugh.

VIC (*to* ROCK). Anyway, you checked 'em all didn't yer?

ROCK (*no response*).

VIC. Did ya?

ROCK (*no response*).

VIC. Sir?

Pause.

CHARMAINE. 'E never done this one, Vic.

VIC. Eh?

Pause. Then CHARMAINE *gasps and springs away from* REX's *wardrobe.* VIC *rises. They gravitate towards each other. Long pause.*

VIC. Shit!!

VIC *and* CHARMAINE *rush to the door.*

CHARMAINE. I can't 'ear nothing.

VIC. No. Very irregular.

CHARMAINE. It is, init?

Pause. ROCK *drifts towards the bathroom.*

VIC. Well, this is a right old two-an'-eight.

CHARMAINE. It's the last time you're doing a favour for anyone.

VIC. Leave off, darlin'.

CHARMAINE. It is, Vic!

VIC. Inasmuch as it was a matter of a friend in need.

CHARMAINE. Some friend! 'E's left us lookin' like a right couple o' monkeys, en' 'e?

VIC. I wish we was monkeys – we could shin down the drainpipe!

CHARMAINE (*giggles. Pause*). I'm 'ungry, Vic – are you?

VIC. Peckish.

CHARMAINE. Is that place up Mount Pleasant open?

VIC. What, Agamenmon?

CHARMAINE. Yeah.

VIC. Yeah, 'e's open till three o'clock in the morning, seven days a week.

CHARMAINE. Oh, that's right. I fancy a kebab.

VIC. I could sink a shish.

Pause.

CHARMAINE. What're we going to do, Vic?

VIC. Well, all we can do is explain what we was doin' 'ere, and bugger off.

CHARMAINE. 'E knows what we was doin' 'ere.

VIC. 'Ow? Oh, bollocks – course 'e does!

CHARMAINE. 'Ere, Vic . . .

VIC. What?

CHARMAINE. What was that I said about 'im?

VIC. I can't remember.

CHARMAINE. I could cut my tongue out.

VIC. It ain't no use in crying over spilt milk; inasmuch sticks and stones; what's done is done; the truth's out; what goes up can't come down; it ain't a jack-in-the-box. Any'ow, let 'e 'oo chucks the first brick be free of guilt, inasmuch people in glass 'ouses shouldn't throw stones. Two wrongs don't make a right!

CHARMAINE. I know that, Vic!

VIC. When in Rome . . . a dog learns by example.

CHARMAINE. You said 'e was a villain.

VIC. No, I never.

CHARMAINE. You did, Vic.

VIC. Not inasmuch. Any'ow, what about what you said about 'is missis?

CHARMAINE. What did I say about 'is missis?

VIC. You said she was a dipsomaniac.

CHARMAINE. I never said that – you said that!

VIC. No, I never!

CHARMAINE. Yes, you did, Vic. I don't even know what it means.

VIC. Course you do!

CHARMAINE. What?

VIC. It means you can't get enough of it.

CHARMAINE. Enough of what?

VIC. You know – bunk-ups.

CHARMAINE. Vic! That's a nymphomaniac!

VIC. Oh, yeah.

Almost simultaneously, they remember ROCK's *presence. Pause.*

VIC. Oh, that's a nice telly, init?

CHARMAINE. Yeah, it is, init?

VIC. State Of The Art! Has it got a Teletext, inasmuch the Oracle? I reckon in a 'undred years' time, tellies'll be so small, you'll be able to clip 'em on your glasses . . . wear 'em while you're drivin' your car! You'll be able to call it, like a dog, "Ere, come 'ere, Telly, there's a good boy . . . turn over, Channel–19, aaah!' You'll be able to cook liver on your pocket microwave.

CHARMAINE. Yeah, well . . . we're all in a state of shock ain't we?

VIC. Inasmuch we're all tarred with the same feather!

CHARMAINE. That's right, Vic. I mean, I know 'e's your Dad, an' you love 'im, right? But 'e is usin' threatening behaviour against us, in'e, Vic?

VIC. That's right. But a man can do what 'e likes in the privacy of 'is own 'ome, inasmuch an Englishman's 'ome is 'is castle, even if it's a prefab. But 'e is performin' a bit preposterous, inasmuch out of order. I bet 'e give you the pip, didn' 'e? inasmuch the willies ('scuse my French) with all that argein' an' bargein' an' shoutin' an' bawlin'?

CHARMAINE. Where's your Mum, eh?

VIC. What's your Dad doin', bakin' a cake?

CHARMAINE. I bet you wish she was 'ere, don't you? (*Going to the bathroom door.*) I wish my Mum was 'ere.

VIC. I know – 'e's been and dumped 'er in Tenerife, in 'e, poor old cow?

CHARMAINE. Vic!!!

VIC. Oh, beg pardon . . .

CHARMAINE (*through door*). 'Ello, darlin' . . . what you doin'?

VIC. What's she up to, eh?

CHARMAINE. She's got a towel over 'er 'ead.

VIC. She's sitting up in the corner like Little Miss Muffet.

CHARMAINE. She's terrified!

VIC. Yeah, course she is – she's like a rabbit.

CHARMAINE. No, she ain't.

VIC. Yeah, she is.

CHARMAINE. Ow?

Pause.

VIC. A rabbit . . . a rabbit . . . strolls out of a 'edge in a country lane . . . mindin' 'is own business in the pitch black; stands in the middle of the road, scratchin' 'is arse, thinkin' about the Meanin' of Life. All of a sudden, without warnin', a car, doin' a thousand miles an hour, 'urtles towards 'im; does 'e 'op it? – no, o' course not: 'e stands there, inasmuch spiflicated. In a trance. Like a moron. Hypnotised. By its 'eadlights. Frozen, like a packet of peas. (*Makes death noise.*) Dead.

CHARMAINE (*to* MELANIE-JANE). What you up to? Eh?

VIC (*to* ROCK). 'T's 'uman nature, ain't it? (*He bangs on the glass door with his torch.*)

CHARMAINE. Vic!!

VIC. She moved!

CHARMAINE. Course she moved!

VIC. Just making sure she ain't paralysed.

CHARMAINE *tuts.*

VIC. Inasmuch she ain't got lockjaw.

Enter REX, *the gun in one hand, a glass of whisky-and-ice in the other.*

REX. Right. That's one crisis dealt with. Nearly got caught short there.

VIC. Are you feeling better in yourself, then, Rex?

REX. Yes, thankyou, Vic.

VIC. Did you nip out there, boss . . . to turn your bike around?

REX. No. There's more than one way to skin a cat.

VIC. Yeah, course. 'Nuff said . . .'

CHARMAINE. It's embarrassing, ain't it, Mr Weasel?

VIC. Course, relieving yourself can put a different colour on things –

CHARMAINE. Yeah.

VIC. – Inasmuch improve your temperament for the better, with all due respects.

REX (*pointing gun at bathroom and Maggotts*). She's still in there.

CHARMAINE *gasps.*

VIC. 'T's alright, darlin'. Sorry we moved, Rex!

REX. What?

CHARMAINE. From the bed, Mr Weasel.

REX (*waving gun*). I want her out!!

VIC. Yeah – course you do!

CHARMAINE. Is this glass shatterproof, Mr Weasel?

REX. I'm not breaking that!

CHARMAINE. Oh, I didn't mean that, I was just –

VIC. Only she's in a bit of a state . . . She's behavin' like . . . a retracted porcupine . . . turned in on itself, and sticking out its egretious prongs . . . inasmuch 'ibernating.

CHARMAINE. I think a cup of tea might bring her round, Mr Weasel.

REX. Oh, you do, do you?

CHARMAINE. Now, I'm not bein' cheeky nor nothing, Mr Weasel, don't get me wrong.

VIC. We was addressin' ourselves to the problem in 'and.

CHARMAINE. That's right, Vic.

VIC. I only 'ope she don't start frothin' at the mouth, get it all

over your carpets there; I can see they're not an offcut
remnant inasmuch as they're worth more than four pounds
fifty a square yard.

REX. No. Has he talked to her yet?

CHARMAINE. No.

VIC. I'm sorry to say young Master Weasel hasn't piped up,
squeaked or burped a syllable.

REX. That's not surprising. How am I going to flush her out?

VIC. Well, I reckon you've got a bit of a problem on your 'ands
'ere, Rex; inasmuch as you're dealing with a Homo Sapiens.
Now if she was a rodent, inasmuch a recalcitrant rat gone to
ground, it would just be a matter of carefully-placed bait-
trays, inasmuch Neo-Serexa.

REX. Neo-Serexa! You're supposed to be using the Klerat.

VIC. I'm sorry, boss, but I reckon the Klerat's overrated.

REX. The Klerat is a one-feed poison.

VIC. Nah – that's what it says on the box!

REX. It is – take it from me.

VIC. But I've got a tub-and-a-half of the Neo in the car.

REX. Well, use it up!

VIC. I'm trying, but there's a shortage of rats up my end.

REX. That's no excuse.

VIC. I'll give 'em a double-dose.

REX. No! – don't you waste it!

VIC. Trouble is, the more you give 'em, the less there are, the
more you got, ad infinitem.

CHARMAINE. I really think a warm, milky drink'd be the best
thing, Mr Weasel.

ROCK. Where's Mum?

REX. Where d'you think she is?

ROCK. I dunno.

REX. Where did we go for Christmas?

ROCK. Lanzarote.

REX. So – where's your mother?

ROCK. I dunno, do I? What're you doing here?

REX. I live here. What are you doing here? Ha, crafty bastard – caught yer! How d'you get in, eh? Who gave you the keys?

ROCK. Mum.

REX. Oh, did she? (*Pause.*) And don't you argue the toss with me, Maggott – you use the Klerat!

Exit ROCK.

REX. Where are you going? (*Follows him to the doorway.*) OI!!!!

The following whispered, quickly and inaudibly.

VIC. What're we goin' a do?

CHARMAINE. Well, I dunno – we can't leave that girl in there.

VIC. But it ain't got nothin' to do with us.

CHARMAINE. Vic, we can't – I'm not leavin' 'er – I'm not!

REX *is standing in the doorway, scrutinising them. They stop. Pause. Then –*

CHARMAINE (*aloud*). I 'ope she's going to be alright.

VIC. Yeah, 'course she is! She's full o' beans! (*Pause.*) Well, if everything's ginger-peachy with you, then, Boss, inasmuch you're clear about it, we'll be off . . .

CHARMAINE. Yeah . . .

VIC. 'Cos the truth is, it isn't what it ain't, 'cos it ain't what it isn't; inasmuch it ain't what it looks like, 'cos it ain't. 'Cos it is what it is, and it ain't what it ain't. Is it? Charmaine?

CHARMAINE. Yeah – no!

Pause. REX *continues his silent scrutiny.* VIC *makes several abortive attempts to start walking out of the room. These are vaguely echoed by* CHARMAINE. *Eventually . . .*

CHARMAINE. So, you just got back tonight, then, Mr Weasel. It's tiring, 'plane-travel, ain't it? I find it.

VIC. Yeah, I bet Rex wants to get to 'is bed – ain't that right, boss?

REX (*going to bed*). Yes, it is.

During the following, REX now puts down his airgun and his drink, and proceeds to prepare his bed by pounding and paddling the pillows. When this is finished, he sits on the bed, and takes off his shoes.

VIC. I reckon you've got a touch of the old jet-lag syndrome, inasmuch as it catches up with you; specially on long-'ops, across the Equator to Australia and such: you can arrive before you've left.

CHARMAINE *giggles.*

VIC. It disturbs your equilibrium. (*Pause.*) Alright, then, boss? If everything's hundred per cent with you, then, inasmuch tickety-boo, we'll be on our way!

CHARMAINE. Remember, that time we come back from Torremolinos, Vic? We was sleepin' nearly all the next day, wan' we?

VIC. Yeah, we was; but that was more to do with the grub and the grog, wan'it?

CHARMAINE. That's right! I was talking stupid then, as well, wan' I?

VIC. Yeah, we was, yeah!!

CHARMAINE (*laughs. Pause*). Are you going to bed, then, Mr Weasel?

REX (*aggressive*). Yes, I am going to bed. Any objections?

CHARMAINE (*good-humoured*). No! I wouldn't mind going to bed myself!

VIC. No need for that, Rex: she's only showin' a bit of concern.

CHARMAINE. It's alright, Vic.

VIC. What?

CHARMAINE. What's she doin'? (*She goes to the bathroom door, and taps on it.*) Listen, darlin': you can't stay in there all night. You've got to come out. What's the matter, eh? You can tell me. (*The rest of this speech from this point is delivered quietly, intimately, and almost inaudibly*). We're pals, ain't we? Mmm? Eh? Remember, we was 'avin' a laugh a few minutes ago – remember? Come on, darlin'. What you goin' a do in there

all night? You won't be able to eat nothin'. Ain't you 'ungry?
Eh? (*Pause.*) 'Ere – what about your Mum? Won't she be
worryin' about you? Eh? (*Pause.*) Listen, darlin' – I know you
think it's a mad'ouse out 'ere, don't yer? Mm? But . . . if you
come out, I'll protect you. I will. (*Pause.*) Honest. Eh? D'you
need anything? I've got some Nurofen in my bag – would
you like one? Please, darlin' – why don't you just come up to
the glass and talk to me? Eh? (*Pause.*) Listen, darlin' . . . it'll
really make my night if you come over 'ere. Come on, come
and talk to me – please. Just for me. Mm?

REX. Is she coming out?

*The following dialogue runs simultaneously with the preceding speech,
and starts when* CHARMAINE *begins to talk quietly.*

VIC. You got a callus there, Rex?

REX. No, Golfer's Foot.

VIC. Ooh, that sounds nasty. I 'ad a verruca once, when I was a
kid. My Mum made me burn my plimsolls.

REX. Did she? That must've stunk.

VIC. They did a bit; they was my big brother's. As a matter of
fact, they was 'is big brother's before that. (*Pause.*) Come to
think of it, I've got a vague recollection my sister wore 'em
one summer. (*Pause.*) I 'ope you didn't get the wrong end of
the stick there, Rex . . . inasmuch when the cat's away, the
mice do play, inasmuch ignorance is bliss, da!! (*Pause.*)
Course, they're a bad design, ain't they, feet? They weren't
built to take the weight of the body in a vertical position;
they was designed to be used in tandem, with the hands, like
a quadruped, scurrying and foraging in the bracken, in a
position, thus. But, what with the Ascent of Man, inasmuch
Evolution, 'e is now able to reach 'igh kitchen units, and
change electric light-bulbs, without the use of too 'igh a step-
ladder. Whereas once, we was as common as the Lowly
Iguana, crawlin', with a vegetarian bent.

REX. Is she coming out?

CHARMAINE. I'm sorry, I'm doin' my best.

REX. Well, get on with it!

CHARMAINE. Alright, Mr Weasel!

VIC. She's 'avin' a go, Rex!

    Pause.

CHARMAINE (*normal audibility*). 'Ello, darlin'! Now . . . can you
    'ear me? If you can 'ear me, tap your foot.

VIC. That's good. (*Pause.*) Anything?

CHARMAINE. I dunno . . .

REX. This is bloody stupid.

VIC. D'y'ave a nice 'oliday, Rex?

    REX *glowers.*

VIC. Only, I've always thought it'd be good to go away for
    Christmas. Save messin' up yer kitchen.

CHARMAINE (*laughing*). 'Ere – when was you ever in a kitchen,
    Vic?

VIC. What about the giblets?

CHARMAINE. Well, you know me and giblets!

VIC. I know all about you and giblets!!

    VIC *and* CHARMAINE *laugh uproariously.* REX *looks from one to
    the other in total incomprehension.*

CHARMAINE. What was 'er name again?

VIC. I can't remember. Shall I ask your boy, boss?

REX. You can try.

VIC. Shall I?

REX. Go on.

VIC. I will.

    Exit VIC. REX *yawns a big yawn, for a moment forgetting*
    CHARMAINE.

VIC (*off, to* ROCK). Eh?

    REX *remembers* CHARMAINE, *and throws her a suspicious glance.*
    She is still looking at MELANIE-JANE. VIC *returns.*

VIC. Nothing.

REX. Typical. Now what?

CHARMAINE. Just a minute. (*Pause.*) What . . . Is . . . Your . . . Name? Mmm? (*Pause.*) I'll tell you what . . . I'll make a little deal with you: if I tell you my name, will you tell me yours? Mm?

VIC. The police do this.

CHARMAINE. My name's Charmaine. (*Sings.*) I wonder why you keep me waiting, (REX *grabs his gun, and jumps up, defensively.*) Charmaine cries, in vain.
I wonder when bluebirds are mating,
Will you come back again?

I wonder, if I keep on praying,
Will our dreams be the same?
I wonder if ever you think of me, too.
I'm waiting, my Charmaine, for you.

Pause.

VIC. That's nice, darlin'. Very soothing.

Long pause.

MELANIE-JANE (*off*). Melanie-Jane Beetles.

VIC. What's she say?

CHARMAINE. Melanie-Jane.

VIC. Yeah!

REX. Talk to 'er!

MELANIE-JANE (*off*). Beetles with two 'e's'. Like 'beetle'.

CHARMAINE. Oh, 'as it?

MELANIE-JANE (*off*). It hasn't got 'e.a.', like the Beatles. It's got two 'e's'. Everybody gets that wrong.

CHARMAINE. Do they?

MELANIE-JANE (*off*). They do. (*Pause.*) Where's Rocky?

CHARMAINE. What?

MELANIE-JANE (*off*). I want to know where Rocky is.

CHARMAINE. Oh, Rocky! 'E's in the sitting-room, I think.

VIC. No, 'e ain't.

CHARMAINE. In 'e?

VIC. Inasmuch 'e's in the scullery.

REX. Shut up, Maggott!!

MELANIE-JANE (*off*). That man's still there!

VIC. I'm goin' – tell 'er I'm goin'.

MELANIE-JANE (*off*). The man with the gun.

CHARMAINE. Oh, that's Mr Weasel. That's your boyfriend's Dad. He's a very nice man.

Pause.

MELANIE-JANE (*off*). I want to speak to Rocky, please.

CHARMAINE. I'll see what I can do, darlin' – don't you worry.

MELANIE-JANE (*off*). But I'm not coming out till that man's gone away. I'm not.

VIC. Medical shock can induce violence.

CHARMAINE. Are you getting the gist of this, Mr Weasel?

REX. Course I am. I'm not deaf. Right. Pay attention. This is the Battle Plan. One: I go in the lounge. Two: you tell her. Three: she comes out. Four: Rock comes in. Five: they talk. Understand?

CHARMAINE. Yes, Mr Weasel.

REX. Got that, Maggott?

VIC. Affirmative, boss.

REX (*momentarily suspicious*). Good. Tell her. (*Exit.*) Rock! Rock!

VIC *rushes over to* CHARMAINE. *The following speeches run simultaneously.*

REX (*off, loudly*). Go and talk to her. (*Pause.*) What're you waiting for? Get in there!

VIC (*inaudibly*). Charmaine; Charmaine! We've got to get out of 'ere. Charmaine, come on! It's nothing to do with us – it's 'is responsibility.

CHARMAINE (*inaudibly*). Listen, darlin', 'e's gone in the other room 'cos Rocky's in there – Vic, just a minute! Ssh! 'E's comin' to talk to you, darlin', so there's nothin' to worry about – Vic!

The following is heard by VIC *and* CHARMAINE, *who have stopped talking.*

REX (*off*). Right! You great lump! Pull yourself together, and bloody well get on with it!!!

REX *thrusts* ROCK *into the room, and disappears off, mumbling.* VIC *and* CHARMAINE *rush over to* ROCK.

CHARMAINE. You alright, darlin'?

VIC. Cor', 'e's a right old bastard, ain't 'e?

CHARMAINE. Don't let 'im walk all over you like that!

VIC. If my old man did that to me, I'd pull 'is eyes out with a corkscrew.

CHARMAINE. It's 'umiliatin'.

VIC. It ain't on.

CHARMAINE. She's very badly shaken up, your little girl.

VIC. Yeah – she's asked for you specifically.

CHARMAINE. You're needed, that's what you are!

VIC. She wants a bit of kindness –

CHARMAINE. That's right.

VIC. – Inasmuch warmth and affection.

CHARMAINE. Come on – use your instincts.

VIC. Yeah – go on.

CHARMAINE. But you've got to be quick about it!

VIC. You're 'er only link with reality.

CHARMAINE. That's right.

VIC. Inasmuch you're the light at the end of 'er tunnel. You're 'er only salvation. She's . . . she's like a lemming, teetering on the edge of the cliff; you've got to reach out your 'and, grab 'old of 'er tail, and drag 'er back!

CHARMAINE. Are you sure you're goin' a be alright?

VIC. Yeah – course 'e will . . . won't yer?

ROCK (*no response*).

VIC. There y'are! Look at 'im: fine, big, strappin' fella!

CHARMAINE. We'll be prayin' for you.

VIC. She will; I won't – I'm an agnostic.

> CHARMAINE *laughs uproariously.*

VIC. Anyway, God bless; Merry Christmas; nice to 'ave met you; good will to all men, inasmuch persons; and Auld Lang Syne.

CHARMAINE. And tell 'er Charmaine was askin' for 'er.

VIC. You've got a right little cracker there.

CHARMAINE. We'll be waiting for our invitations to the wedding, won't we, Vic?

VIC (*good-humoured*). Shut up, Charmaine!

> CHARMAINE *laughs.*

> *Enter* REX.

REX. What's going on?

VIC. We was just goin' 'ome, Rex.

CHARMAINE. Thank you very much, Mr Weasel.

VIC. If it's alright with you, we'll be making tracks.

CHARMAINE. Yeah.

REX. She's still in there!

CHARMAINE. Is she?

VIC. Oh, yeah!

> *Exit* VIC *and* CHARMAINE.

REX. Listen, fairy: get your playmate out of my bog!!!

> *Exit* REX.

> *During the following offstage dialogue,* ROCK *stands and looks at the bathroom door. Eventually,* MELANIE-JANE *opens it slightly, and gestures to* ROCK *through the gap. Then she opens it a little further, and hovers on the threshold. Thus they gaze at each other helplessly across the room.*

REX (*off*). Oi, you two! Sit down!

VIC (*off*). 'Ow d'you mean, Rex?

REX (*off*). Make yourselves at home!

CHARMAINE (*off*). It's alright – really, Mr Weasel.

REX (*off*). Right, Mrs Maggott, you'll have a sherry. What do you want, Vic?

VIC (*off*). No, it's alright, Rex.

REX (*off*). Scotch, Bourbon, Rye?

VIC (*off*). Got any whisky?

REX (*off*). Yes!

CHARMAINE (*off*). I thought we was goin' 'ome, Vic.

VIC (*off*). No, it's alright, Rex – really, yeah, three's a crowd, five's a rabble.

CHARMAINE (*off*). I have to be up early in the morning, Mr Weasel.

REX (*off*). One sherry, one Scotch.

CHARMAINE (*off*). No thankyou, Mr Weasel.

REX (*off*). Go on, you'll like it. Here you are, Vic.

VIC (*off*). Well, that's very civil of you, Rex, under the circumstances.

REX (*off*). Here's your sherry.

CHARMAINE (*off*). Are you having a drink, Vic?

VIC (*off*). We'll 'ave one for the road – eh?

CHARMAINE (*off*). Well, I'll have one if you're having one, but I shouldn't mix my drinks.

REX (*off*). Right: Merry Bloody Christmas!!

VIC (*off*). Chin-chin!

Pause.

CHARMAINE (*off*). I think boys get on better with their Mums, Mr Weasel, don't you? I mean, Vic, 'e gets on better with 'is Mum.

VIC (*off*). I do.

REX (*off*). Do you?

VIC (*off*). Yeah, I do.

CHARMAINE (*off*). I feel sorry for young people these days, though, Mr Weasel. There's not enough places for them to go. And I don't think we communicate enough with them, d'you know what I mean? I watch 'Top of the Pops' every Thursday night so's I've got something to say to my niece and nephew – it's like a labour of love with me, d'you know what I mean?

VIC (*off*). My wife is an acute observer of the Human Animal . . . inasmuch she is a student of the University of Life.

CHARMAINE (*off*). I'm not smart nor nothing, but I do know a thing or two about people.

VIC (*off*). Yeah, she's an instinctive, inasmuch a man-watcher.

CHARMAINE (*off: laughs*.)

VIC (*off*). No, I know, not, not, er –

CHARMAINE (*off*). No, I know, I –

VIC (*off*). I know I'm the only man you ever wanna watch.

CHARMAINE (*off*). Oh, that's what you think!

VIC (*off: laughs loudly and uproariously*.)

REX (*off*). Shut up, Maggot!!!! (*Pause*.) Go and see what's going on in there, will you?

MELANIE-JANE *hears this, and runs back into the bathroom, without closing the door*.

CHARMAINE (*off*). Are you talking to me, Mr Weasel?

REX (*off*). Yes. If you wouldn't mind.

CHARMAINE (*off*). I'll do that for you.

Enter CHARMAINE. *Only mouthing her words, she conducts a brief, friendly one-sided interview with* ROCK, *in which she ascertains his and* MELANIE-JANE's *condition, reassures him, and announces that she is going to close the door. She does this, giving him a conspiratorial wink on the way out.*

ROCK *stands motionless, looking at the bathroom. Pause.*
MELANIE-JANE *appears, and rushes across the room into his arms.*
She does this with such velocity that she almost knocks him over. Pause.
He turns round, and keeping his eye fixed on the door, he backs away
from it with MELANIE-JANE *still hugging him, like a koala-bear or*
a leech. Pause. MELANIE-JANE *now hugs him more passionately,*
and buries her head in his chest. She sinks to the floor, and hugs one of
his legs caressing it fervently for a while. Then she climbs up him
gradually, eventually (when she is standing) putting her arms round
him; he doesn't respond, so she puts his arms round her, one after the
other. Suddenly, they kiss, passionately, uninhibitedly, mutually; then,
just as suddenly, ROCK *pulls away.* MELANIE-JANE *rushes about*
the room like an uncoiled spring, whilst ROCK *watches the door.*
Then, again suddenly, they come back together embracing and kissing –
a long, passionate kiss. For a moment, they stop, and ROCK *picks up*
MELANIE-JANE, *sweeping her off the floor, and bears her to the*
bed, on to which they both sink, resuming their kiss. MELANIE-
JANE *stops kissing for a moment.*

MELANIE-JANE. Just a minute . . .

She takes off her glasses. They resume their kiss. Pause. Enter REX
. . .

The following dialogue runs simultaneously with the above action,
starting as CHARMAINE *rejoins* REX *and* VIC, *having closed the*
door.

REX (*off*). What's going on?

CHARMAINE (*off*). It's alright.

REX (*off*). Has she come out?

CHARMAINE (*off*). Yeah.

REX (*off*). Is the door open?

CHARMAINE (*off*). Yeah.

REX (*off*). Right – we'll give 'em a couple o'minutes.

Pause.

CHARMAINE (*off*). This is a nice sherry, Mr Weasel.

REX (*off*). Yeah, yeah – it's a good one.

VIC (*off*). Ditto the Scotch.

CHARMAINE (*off*). We nearly drunk all our Christmas drink, in't we, Vic?

VIC (*off*). Yeah, we 'ave – put a 'ole in it, 'aven't we?

CHARMAINE *laughs (off*).

Pause.

VIC (*off*). I don't know why, but Christmas always makes me think of the War.

CHARMAINE (*off*). Why's that, Vic?

VIC (*off*). I dunno – I weren't in it or nothing; I ain't old enough.

CHARMAINE (*off*). Yeah . . . you seen it on telly, though.

VIC (*off*). I've seen it on telly. I've read a lot about it.

CHARMAINE (*off*). Yeah. Vic loves 'is books, Mr Weasel.

VIC (*off*). I do, yeah . . . yeah. (*Pause.*) No, it's all the old people down the market when I was a kid. They used to talk about it like it was still 'appening . . . they made me feel like I was in the Blitz.

CHARMAINE (*off*). I'm glad you wasn't, Vic.

VIC (*off*). Yeah, so'm I. (*Pause.*) Then, of course, there was old Lord Ha-Ha, wasn't there?

CHARMAINE (*off*). Oh, yeah . . .

VIC (*off*). Yeah. 'E was an Englishman, living in Germany, and working for the German BBC. Broadcasting propaganda to the Home Front . . . (*Imitating William Joyce, not very accurately.*) 'Germany calling! Germany calling! Mrs Smith! Do not send Johnny to the War! Keep him at home, tied to your apron strings . . .' That's 'ow 'e used to go on. 'Otherwise he will be crushed by the Might of the Reich!' Then, of course, a lot of young men went into the Black Market.

CHARMAINE (*off*). That's right.

VIC (*off*). Selling stockings; instead of fighting in the trenches.

CHARMAINE (*off*). Ow'd they know which Mrs Smith 'e was talkin' to?

VIC (*off*). Well, 'e wasn't talking to A Mrs Smith in particular, inasmuch as it's the way we would say, 'Mrs Schmidt.'

CHARMAINE (*off*). Oh, yeah.

Pause.

VIC (*off*). Course, a lot o' people used to sleep in the tube-stations, didn't they?

CHARMAINE (*off*). That's right. Shelterin'.

VIC (*off*). Yeah.

CHARMAINE (*off*). Done a lot o' singing down there.

VIC (*off*). They did, yeah – 'eld 'em together. But it was very inconvenient for the traveller; gettin' out of the train, steppin' on their 'eads . . .

Pause.

CHARMAINE (*off*). Yeah . . .

VIC (*singing, off*). Run, rabbit, run rabbit,
                    Run, run, run . . .

CHARMAINE (*off*). That's right, Vic. They'll be alright, Mr Weasel.

Pause.

VIC (*off*). Course, if there was a war now, it'd be different, wouldn't it? Be nucelar.

CHARMAINE (*off*). Yeah.

VIC (*off*). Be nothing left . . . unless o' course they dropped the neutron bomb.

CHARMAINE (*off*). Oh, I don't think Mr Weasel wants to hear about that, Vic!

VIC (*off*). That's the bomb that kills people but saves property . . . and clothing.

REX, *who has not been listening to any of this, now enters the bedroom;* ROCK *and* MELANIE-JANE *are too involved to notice him. Short pause.*

REX. You cheeky buggers!!

ROCK *leaps off the bed.* MELANIE-JANE *sits up.*

REX. Well, well, well!!! If it wasn't my bed you were on, I'd apologise. Are you going to introduce me? I'm Rocky's

Daddy! (*Pause.*) And this is my bedroom.

MELANIE-JANE (*getting up*). It's a very big bedroom, Mr Weasel.

REX. I'm glad you like it. (*He picks up her glasses.*) These yours?

MELANIE-JANE. Thank you very much. (*Pause.*) I'm very sorry . . .

REX. Well?

ROCK (*no response*).

REX. Does he talk to you? He never says a flaming word to me.
He hasn't said a dicky-bird since the day he was born. Still . . .

VIC *and* CHARMAINE *have appeared in the doorway.* VIC *knocks
on the door, pom-diddly-om-pom; pom-pom.*

VIC. 'Scuse me, Rex; only me and Charmaine was thinkin' about
wending our weary way. (*Pause.*) And by dint of farewell, I'd
just like to say, 'Thankyou very much for all your 'ospitality.'
Which, under the circumstances, was completely
unwarranted, what with all the various disturbances. So,
Thankyou Very Much. (*Pause.*) 'Appy Christmas. (Although
it's almost over.) H'au revoir, inasmuch, Goodbye . . .

CHARMAINE. We don't want to outstay our welcome. 'Cos it is
a family time, Christmas, init?

VIC. Yeah, it is, yeah. (*Pause.*) Er . . .

CHARMAINE. You're lookin' a lot better, ain't she, Vic?

VIC. Yeah, got a bit of colour back in your cheeks.

CHARMAINE. She's got a lovely smile!

VIC. She's a pretty girl, ain't she?

CHARMAINE. Yeah. (*To* ROCK.) You done a good job there.

VIC. Yeah, well done! 'Andsome young couple, ain't they?

CHARMAINE. Yeah.

Pause.

VIC. Er . . . sh' we . . .?

CHARMAINE. } Yeah.
VIC.   { Yeah.

CHARMAINE. Ba-bye.

VIC. Bye, then.

CHARMAINE. Ba-bye.

MELANIE-JANE. Bye-bye.

VIC. 'T's alright, we'll see ourselves out, Rex.

Exit VIC *and* CHARMAINE. *Pause. Then* REX *goes to the door.*

REX. Oi! Maggott!! Come back 'ere a minute!!

He stays at the door for a moment, then returns to where he was. Pause. VIC *appears.*

VIC. What's up, Rex? Found someone in the cupboard? (*Laughs.*)

REX. How long were you in prison, Vic?

Pause.

VIC. What're you talkin' about? That was 'undreds o' years ago.

REX. What did they get you for, G.B.H.?

VIC. Nah! Any'ow, it wasn't prison, inasmuch as it was Borstal.

REX. Oh, was it?

VIC. Yeah!

REX. Well, what were you doing, then, nicking motors?

VIC. Nah!

CHARMAINE. Vic was framed, Mr Weasel.

REX. I'm sure he was!

CHARMAINE. He was!

VIC. I bleedin' was! I fell in with a bad lot, inasmuch they took me for a mug; told me they was out for a laugh, ended up burnin' down a ware'ouse, inasmuch three hundred thousand poundsworth of fur coats.

CHARMAINE. Yeah – Vic was left alone to take the rap. And 'e didn't get no 'elp from 'is Dad, neether.

VIC. Dead right!

REX. Why don't I know about this?

VIC. With all due respects, boss, it ain't none of your bleedin' business!

CHARMAINE. I think that's Vic's own personal concern, Mr Weasel.

REX. Did they put you inside, as well?

CHARMAINE. I beg your pardon?

REX. You do have a criminal record?

CHARMAINE. I do not!

VIC. Now 'ang on a minute, Rex! You're takin' bleedin' liberties. You can 'ave a go at me, 'cos I work for yer, but you leave my missis out o' this!!

REX. Did you enjoy my chocolate, Mrs Maggott?

VIC. What?!

Pause.

CHARMAINE. Now, look 'ere, Mr Weasel.

REX. Yes?

CHARMAINE. I've 'ad just about enough of this.

REX. Oh, have you?

CHARMAINE. I have, I'm not one to speak out of turn, but I 'ave to say something. We've been made fools of, Vic an' me. We come 'ere tonight with the best of intentions. We live a quiet life. We work all the year round for not very much money; and, come Christmas, we like to enjoy ourselves, 'ave a few drinks and a laugh. We've been to one party . . . I know I was talkin' stupid, but we all do when we've 'ad a few.

VIC. Course we do.

CHARMAINE. But I do not see why we 'ave to be treated like little kids!

VIC. It's alright, darlin' – don't get yourself upset.

CHARMAINE. I'm alright, Vic. We've been led up the garden path like lambs to the slaughter, we 'ave. Let's go, Vic.

CHARMAINE *starts to exit.*

REX. Alright I believe you – thousands wouldn't.

VIC. Good! 'Cos you should; 'cos it's the whole truth; the 'ole truth, and nothing but the truth! And that's 'ow it stands!

REX. Alright, don't you start sounding off, as well!

CHARMAINE. Leave it, Vic.

VIC. Eh?

REX (*to* ROCK). WHAT ARE YOU STARING AT??!!

VIC. Why don't you fuckin' leave 'im alone, you big bully?!

CHARMAINE. Vic!!

Pause.

REX (*quietly*). Watch your mouth, Vic. (*Pause.*) Now, I appreciate your coming round here this evening.

VIC. Oh, do yer?!

REX. Yes, I do. And you'll find a token of my appreciation in your pay packet at the end of the month.

VIC. What's that, me cards?

REX. No, a little extra.

VIC. Extra what?

REX. Extra money.

Pause.

VIC. Nah. No, that ain't necessary, Rex.

REX. I know it's not.

VIC. Nah. No, you're . . . you're well out of order, Rex.

REX. You scratch my back, I'll scratch yours.

CHARMAINE. Come on, Vic.

REX. When are you back at work, Vic?

VIC. Tuesday. Cockroaches in Colindale.

REX. Oh, yes. You can have a lie-in tomorrow.

VIC. Oh, thanks very much.

CHARMAINE. It's a Bank Holiday anyway, Vic.

VIC. Oh, yeah.

REX. Come on, I'll see you out.

CHARMAINE. *(to the others)*. Take care.

VIC. 'Bye.

MELANIE-JANE. Bye-bye.

> *Exit* REX, VIC *and* CHARMAINE. *During the following dialogue,* MELANIE-JANE *tries unsuccessfully to communicate with* ROCK.

VIC *(off)*. Oh – yer keys.

REX *(off)*. No, I don't want 'em – give 'em to Roy.

VIC *(off)*. Fair enough.

REX *(off)*. Mind how you drive.

VIC *(off)*. No problem.

REX *(off)*. The police are out.

VIC *(off)*. I'm as sober as a judge.

REX *(off)*. It's that time of year.

CHARMAINE *(off)*. Gone nippy, init?

VIC *(off: opening front door)*. 'Ere y'are, darlin'.

CHARMAINE *(off)*. Goodnight, Mr Weasel.

REX *(off)*. Goodnight, Mrs Maggott.

VIC *(off)*. Goodnight, Rex.

REX *(off)*. Goodnight, Vic.

VIC *(off)*. 'Appy New Year!

> *The front door closes. Enter* REX. *He is still holding the airgun. Pause.*

REX. Any questions?

ROCK *(no response)*.

REX. Eh?

> *Long pause.* REX *looks round the room, his attention eventually focusing on the soft animals on the floor. He stares at these violently for a long time. Then he stares at* ROCK. ROCK *stares back. Then –*

ROCK. WHAT?!!

Pause. Then REX *moves quickly towards the bathroom;* MELANIE-JANE *jumps out of his way.*

MELANIE-JANE. Don't – !!!

REX *goes into the bathroom, and reappears with his dressing-gown and his toilet-bag. He puts them on the bed. He puts the gun on the bed. He goes to the chest of drawers, and takes out a pair of pyjamas which he puts on the bed. He goes out, and returns with a full bottle of Scotch whisky . He sits on the bed, and puts on his shoes. During this –*

MELANIE-JANE. It makes you burp . . . whisky. (*Pause.*) It's a shame you can't walk home anymore. It's not safe. But then it might not really be safe getting a taxi, either. You could get raped . . .

REX *has put on his shoes, and now goes to one of the wardrobes, and takes out a leather overnight bag – not part of the luggage he arrived with. He takes this to the bed, and proceeds to pack.*

MELANIE-JANE. Are you going back to Lanzarote, Mr Weasel?

REX *finishes the packing, and zips up the bag. Then he goes to 'his' wardrobe, takes out the raincoat he arrived in, and proceeds to put it on.*

MELANIE-JANE. That's a nice raincoat, Mr Weasel. Hasn't your Daddy got a nice raincoat, Rocky?

ROCK (*no response*).

MELANIE-JANE. Sensible coat.

REX *takes a huge wad of paper money out of his back pocket. He flicks through it.*

REX. D'you need any money?

ROCK (*no response*).

Pause. REX *glances at* MELANIE-JANE, *incidentally.*

MELANIE-JANE. No, thankyou.

REX *ignores this. He counts out some money, and puts it on the bed, under the airgun.*

REX. A hundred quid. (*He goes to the door.*) Have fun.

Exit REX, *closing the door. The front door slams.* MELANIE-JANE *runs to* ROCK, *and stands beside him. Pause.*

MELANIE-JANE. Was that the front door? (*Pause.*) Was it? (*Pause.*) He's hiding – he hasn't gone anywhere. (*Pause. She goes to the door and listens.*) Can't hear anything. (*She opens the door, and creeps into the hall; after a moment, she returns.*) There's nobody here at all. (*Pause, she sits on the bed.*) I thought he was really going to kill us. He left you all that money. (*Pause.*) It's gone all quiet.

ROCK *crosses the room. He stands for a short while, and then crosses back.* MELANIE-JANE *goes out of the room, and returns with her coat and her handbag, which she puts on the bed. She proceeds to put on her coat.*

MELANIE-JANE. My Daddy will murder me. (*Pause.*) What are you going to spend your hundred pounds on? Where is she, your Mummy? What's the matter?

ROCK *moves to the dressing-table, and stares at it.*

MELANIE-JANE. You'd better put it somewhere safe. (*Pause.*) *Do* you like me? (*Pause.*) Are you going to stay here tonight? I bet my Daddy will be in bed by now. No-one will know what time I get in. (*Pause.*) It's a good thing we haven't got a dog. (*Pause.*) Rocky . . .

ROCK *puts on his coat, takes his cassette out of the radio/cassette player and puts it back in his Walkman.*

MELANIE-JANE. Rocky – what are you doing?

Exit ROCK, *quickly. He leaves the flat.*

MELANIE-JANE. Where are you going? (*She follows him to the door.*) What's wrong? (*She rushes back to get her bag, and rushes out.*) Don't go! What about your money? – Rocky: WAIT! (*Off.*) You've left the lights on! (*The front door slams. We hear her beyond it.*) Wait for me! Please . . .!

Long pause. Slow fade to blackout.

The End